1 MONTH OF
FREE
READING

at

www.ForgottenBooks.com

By purchasing this book you are eligible for one month membership to ForgottenBooks.com, giving you unlimited access to our entire collection of over 1,000,000 titles via our web site and mobile apps.

To claim your free month visit: www.forgottenbooks.com/free879233

ISBN 978-0-266-71143-8
PIBN 10879233

For support please visit www.forgottenbooks.com

THE STATE

OF THE

CHURCH AND THE WORLD,

AT THE

FINAL OUTBREAK OF EVIL, AND REVELATION OF ANTICHRIST,

HIS DESTRUCTION AT THE SECOND COMING OF CHRIST

AND THE

USHERING IN OF THE MILLENNIUM.

BY THE

REV. J. G. GREGORY, M. A.

WITH AN

APPENDIX BY MRS. A. P. JOLIFFE.

REPRINTED FROM THE LONDON EDITION.

PHILADELPHIA:

JAMES S. CLAXTON,

SUCCESSOR TO WM. S. & ALFRED MARTIEN,

1214 CHESTNUT STREET.

1867.

CONTENTS.

---

(5)

6 CONTENTS.

PREFACE.

I AM truly conscious of defects in this work, both great and many, which the critic will discover readily. But let him not be too severe; let him believe, rather, that my object is the spiritual welfare of our fellow-christians; and let him deal with me in that spirit of forbearance which such kind belief so readily begets.

And, I pray Almighty God that He will give His blessing to this little work, and pardon all erroneous dealings with the deeper things of His Inspired Word. May He in mercy grant that both the Writer and the Reader, being strengthened by whatever has been written in accordance with His Will, may be guided safely through the trying periods which remain of this "Earth's Eventide," and be led onwards to the dawning of that glorious Day in which the servants of the Lord, who have been waiting for His Advent, shall shine forth in brightness like the Sun, and dwell before the Throne of the eternal King of Kings, in THE UNCEASING GLORY OF THE NEW JERUSALEM.

THE CHURCH AND THE WORLD.

CHAPTER I.

WATCH AND PRAY, FOR THE COMING OF THE LORD DRAWETH NEAR.

We have, also, a more sure word of Prophecy, whereunto ye do well that ye take heed, as unto a light that shineth in a dark place, until the day dawn, and the day-star arise in your hearts.
—2 PETER i. 19.

WE are told, on every side, that we are living in remarkable times. We read of it in the newspapers; we hear it in our daily conversation; and we feel it to be true. There is, undoubtedly, a rumbling of some extraordinary earthquake, which, growing more and more distinct, forewarns the thoughtful that a crisis of no slight importance is not far in our advance. We see, indeed, the Christian, the unbeliever, the philanthropist, and the politician, all agreeing in the expectation of some gigantic outburst. We find the hearts of men of judgment "failing them for fear, and for looking after those things which are coming on the earth." The eyes of many turn with anxious gaze towards the observers of the times, the learned, the statesmen, the merchants, and the ministers of the gospel, with the inquiry—"Watchman, what of the night?" But who among the sons of men can *satisfy* the inquiry? Opinions, various enough, come forth. A rush of many voices gives reply. But who is to be trusted? The only safe

2

response which any man can give, is this—"It is not for you to know the times and the seasons which the Father hath put in His own power." Yet, for all this, there is *a ray of light*, feeble certainly, but not to be neglected, for it comes down directly from that Father's hand of love, and sheds its gentle beam upon this wondrous period in which we live. By this *one* beam, those men who have the spirit of the Lord can read a word of warning, which diffuses joyful expectation through their willing hearts. That word is, "WATCH AND PRAY, FOR THE COMING OF THE LORD DRAWS NEAR." This ray of light illuminates, moreover, a few *signs* and *portents*, and exhorts, "WHEN THESE THINGS BEGIN TO COME TO PASS, THEN LOOK UP AND LIFT YOUR HEADS, FOR YOUR REDEMPTION DRAWETH NIGH.* Now for this gleam let those of us who know the Saviour render praise; and while we read, and watch, and pray, be humble, looking to the Lord submissively, with patient, waiting hearts; behaving ourselves always circumspectly; being well prepared to leave this bondage whensoever our Redeemer's voice shall call us to arise and meet Him.

I know that there are Christians, not a few, who will agree with me that these are times which ought to lead God's people to be much upon the watch-tower, forasmuch as many things betoken clearly that the coming of the Lord is near. And, doubtless, there are others who, although, perhaps, they will not go with me so far as this, will yet agree that these are days when things around forebode a crisis which has scarcely known a precedent. I, therefore,

* Luke xxi. 28.

confidently ask for the attention of my brethren in Christ, to the *heart-stirring* and *important* subject of those prophecies which concern THE FUTURE OF OUR WORLD, and cast a special light upon the SECOND ADVENT OF OUR LORD AND SAVIOUR.

Now, inasmuch as these prophecies have been, till lately, studied by so very few, even among really Christian people, I ought, perhaps, before I speak directly upon the subject, to note carefully THE DUTY which unquestionably lies upon every one of us, to give them *an attention just as close as that we should afford to any other part of Holy Scripture.*

To this duty our text plainly calls attention. Let us observe its language. The "WORD OF PROPHECY" of which it speaks (as we are informed by the twentieth verse) is contained in "THE SCRIPTURES." It is called a "SURE WORD OF PROPHECY;" MORE sure (as the context also shows us,) than the word which the Apostles spoke when they "made known the power and coming of our Lord Jesus Christ; though they had been eye-witnesses of his Majesty."* Again, it is compared to "a light that shineth in a dark place;" wherefore also the Lord's people are expressly told that they "DO WELL," that they "TAKE HEED" to it. And this, not just *occasionally*, but "UNTIL THE DAY DAWN, AND THE DAY-STAR ARISE IN THEIR HEARTS."

With our text, then, for a witness, let us behold the Prophecies of Scripture as "A SURE WORD," on which we may repose our confidence: not as they are deemed by some, a word to be *laid by* at once, as

---

* 2 Peter i. 16.

highly figurative and *incomprehensibly mysterious;*
unfit, therefore, for profitable study. Let us view
them as a LIGHT sent for the illumination of the sincere inquirer, to be used as a continual guide by the
Lord's earnest servants while they sojourn in the
"dark place" of this life's pilgrimage: and let us
avail ourselves unceasingly of prophecy's much-
needed beams, until the night which is "far spent"
shall pass away, and the great "day" of light and
life so long foretold shall "dawn."

But now I well could think I hear already the
objection—"Is it not *unduly inquisitive*, and therefore *wrong*, to search out the momentous matters
which are yet before us in the future?" Does not
the Lord intend rather that the prophecies should be
studied AFTER THE EVENTS WHICH THEY PREDICT
HAVE TRANSPIRED, so that His truth may be con-
firmed, and his faithfulness made known? This is
an objection which lays firm hold upon the minds of
not a few: so that we continually hear it said, that
while *fulfilled* prophecy is of great utility, proving
beyond controversy the foreknowledge, power, judgment, mercy, and deity of God, *unfulfilled* prophecy
had far better be passed over for the present, lest we
be found sinfully prying into those secret things
which belong only to the Lord. Now in reply to
this, we may again refer to the plain language of our
text. The light of prophecy there spoken of, and to
which it is said we "*do* WELL *that we take heed,*" is
not certainly a light prepared by God to cast its
beams upon the path in which a man *has* trodden
hitherto; for, mark the language,—"*Whereunto ye*

do well that ye take heed, as unto a light that shineth in a dark place, UNTIL THE DAY DAWN." This surely speaks with plainness. It is a light which shines as from a guiding lamp, to show the traveller *where he is,* and *what is before him.* But let me give you Bishop Newton's words upon our text. He says, "St. Peter is asserting and establishing the truth of Christ's second coming in power and great glory. (*For we have not followed cunningly-devised fables, when we made known unto you the power and coming of our Lord Jesus Christ, but were eye-witnesses of His Majesty.*) One illustrious proof of His coming in power and glory was His appearing in glory and majesty at His transfiguration. (*For He received from God the Father honor and glory, when there came such a voice to Him from the excellent glory— This is my beloved Son, in whom I am well pleased— and this voice, which came from heaven, we heard when we were with Him in the Holy Mount.*) His appearing once in power and great glory is a good argument that he *may* appear again in like manner; and that He not only *may,* but WILL, we have the further assurance of PROPHECY; (*we have also a more sure word of Prophecy, whereunto ye do well that ye take heed.*)"

With the testimony of a scholar and divine so able, we might well rest satisfied, even were the connection in which the passage stands less plain, and be confident that the "sure word of Prophecy" before us is a word which has its great concern with *an important future;* even with THAT DAY OF WONDERS WHEN THE GREAT "REDEEMER SHALL RETURN AND COME TO

Zion" to be glorified of all. But it is not only our text, with its surrounding context, which gives evidence that we "do well that we take heed" to the "sure word of Prophecy" with reference to things to come. We may take notice also of our Lord's own words. What could he mean but to advise his people thus, when he said *"There shall be signs in the sun, and in the moon, and in the stars, and upon the earth distress of nations with perplexity; the sea and the waves roaring; men's hearts failing them for fear, and for the looking after those things which are coming on the earth. . . . . When these things* BEGIN *to come to pass, then look up and lift up your heads, for your redemption draweth nigh!"** What could our Saviour mean when he spoke these words—but to warn His disciples—*then* and *now*, and to teach them to look forward, marking well the signs of the times, that they might perceive when they are drawing near that glorious period to which He taught them to look forward. It *could* not be that they might profit thereby after the event,—*after* the Lord's coming,— *after* they should have received the inheritance. It *must* have been that they might be *in readiness*, with their loins girt about, and their lamps burning, and they themselves like servants watching for their Lord. I have read somewhere much as follows: If the use of unfulfilled prophecy be *after* the event which it foretells has come to pass, it must be either to the *Lord's people* or to *wicked people* that it is found useful. Now it *cannot* be of any use to the *wicked*. It must needs be *too late* to be of use to

* Luke xxi. 25, 28.

them, when its predictions have received accomplishment in their destruction. The *flood* proved the truth of the Lord's word which Noah delivered; but it certainly was too late to be of any use to the *wicked people* to whom Noah preached; and the *Lord's servants* had *no need* of such a proof as the fulfilment of the prophecy afforded, for they were well aware beforetime that God spoke in faithfulness and truth. Moreover the wicked perished in the flood "*because they did not believe the prophecy* BEFORE *its accomplishment,* and the family of Noah were only saved *because they did believe it.*"

Surely then as the inspired John declares concerning the Apocalypse, so *we* may assert respecting every other prophecy which the Word of God brings forward, "*Blessed is he that readeth, and they that hear the words of this Prophecy, and keep those things which are written therein.*"* So reading and so hearing we shall not fall under the condemnation of the Jews of old—" *Ye hypocrites! ye can discern the face of the sky and of the earth; but how is it that ye do not discern this time?*"†

The objection then which many have advanced upon the ground of a supposed *undue inquisitiveness* is idle.

But let us weigh another prominent objection. An objection raised by many good and seriously-minded Christians. "Do but observe," they say "how great the number of those students of the unfilfilled prophecies who have made shipwreck! Moreover, see the differences which exist among those students who still

---

* Rev. i. 3.   † Luke xii. 56.

stand their ground! Surely such a dangerous, or at least unsatisfactory subject ought to be avoided." Now, allowing that many have made shipwreck, and allowing that great differences of interpretation do exist (though I do not altogether receive the statement as correct), surely prophecy is *not the only subject of great moment* which has become a stumbling-block, or concerning which there have been serious differences of opinion. Satan has been very busy in spreading error with regard to *every* spiritual matter, and his work has told with fearful power on many who were looked upon as the Lord's people. Indeed the very GOSPEL OF SALVATION, which a man *must needs* receive or perish everlastingly, has been made a theme of study by vast numbers who have lacked the spirit of the Lord, and so has proved "A savour of death unto death to their souls." Amazing truth! yet truth indeed! Men have heard and read the GOSPEL OF SALVATION to their own DESTRUCTION!! But shall the Gospel therefore be a subject we forbid? Shall we keep it from our less learned brethren? From our families, our neighbors, our poor? Oh, not so, surely; though it be true that, as in Peter's day, so *now also*, men "wrest the Scriptures to their own destruction." For where can be the cause for fear as to those students of the word who read with humble, self-distrustful hearts, since God has promised that He "will give His Holy Spirit unto them that ask Him."* "If any man," then, shall "lack wisdom" (and who lacks it not?) "let him ask of God who giveth to all men liberally

* Luke xi. 13.

and upbraideth not, and it shall be given him: but let him ask in faith nothing wavering."* So, let us conclude that there is help at hand; and when God plainly tells us—"Search the Scriptures:"† All Scripture is given by inspiration of God, and is profitable. . . . . that the man of God may be perfect:"‡ "Blessed is he that readeth and they that hear the words of this Prophecy:"§ "We have a more sure word of Prophecy whereunto ye do well that ye take heed:" we are not to shrink back, saying as it were, "Lord there are many parts of Scripture I am afraid to study, lest I may be led thereby to error:" but rather in a manner acceptable before the Lord, we are TO DO AS HE HAS BIDDEN, WITHOUT GAINSAYING, and avail ourselves with gratitude of the high privilege which in his word He offers us.

So far then for this objection also. And now, if no antagonist *more powerful* than these arise: (and I know of none more powerful), we may, I think beyond a doubt decide that it is our BOUNDEN DUTY, as those servants who await their Lord's return—*to study* UNFULFILLED PROPHECY.

It will not be right for me to quit the subject of this duty, without adding a few serious words as to the MANNER *in which the study of unfulfilled prophecy should be conducted.*

The students of prophecy are actuated by a diversity of motives:—Some study to obtain food for an imaginative fancy. None are more likely

---

* James i. 5, 6. † John v. 39.
‡ 2 Timothy iii. 16, 17. § Rev. i. 3.

than these to reap error; for the object of God's Word is not to feast the imagination, but to save, establish, and comfort the immortal soul. Others study for the enjoyment of sublime language and splendid imagery, of which the inspired prophecies are full. These also are unlikely to arrive at truth: for God did not give His Word to gratify the taste, but to edify the spirit.

But we need not enumerate farther;—except perhaps to note that there are also those who read and study meekly, prayerfully, and with a view to obtain instruction in those things which God has deemed it right to offer for the contemplation of His people; so that they may be in readiness when the great day of God approaches, and "be found worthy to escape those things which are coming upon the earth, and to stand before the Son of Man."* Such students have a blessing. They will be instructed by the Spirit: as it is written, "They shall all be taught of God:"† and they will not be allowed to fall materially into error. But again—It cannot but be noticed with regret that the *attitude* which is assumed by some of the more careful and sincere students of the prophecies is anything but seemly for poor erring mortals such as we are, when they deal with the deep mysteries of God. We find them making *positive assertions* as to things which are still veiled from human sight: advancing questionable theories, and adhering to them as if in all the world there were no men of judgment to be found, themselves excepted: dealing with prophetic symbols, dates, and parables,

* Luke xxi. 36.   † John vi. 45.

with a positiveness which savors not by any means of Christian humility. *Now let us not act like them.* But rather, while we *never shrink* from reading, hearing or studying *any portion* of God's Word, which He has given for our learning: while we *use* that word in all its parts; its histories, its psalms, its laws, its gospel, and its *prophecies:* while we observe prophetic *images* and *symbols* and *parables* and *dates;* let us not *dare* in any case which bears upon the future, to assert with positiveness that at such and such a time *this incident* or *that* shall come to pass: unless indeed we have *no room* for doubt by reason of the plainness of expression God has used concerning it. Such plainness of expression with regard to the prophetic *dates*—however—*no where*— I believe—occurs; but rather—with regard to every incident *yet future*, it is clearly intimated that " Of that day and that hour knoweth no man."* The time *may* come, and perhaps is *near at hand already*, when we shall be in a position to use the mysterious periods both of Daniel and the Apocalypse with greater certainty.† But for the present, although (as we shall see in the course of these chapters) they are of *great utility* to the waiting and watching Christian, yet we cannot with anything like certainty determine their respective limits.

Avoiding then *all positive assertion* as to those things still in mystery; let us use whatever God has put before us in those Holy Scriptures He has given for **our** learning, with all humility and reverence,

---

* Matt. xxiv. 36. Mark xiii. 32, 33.
† Compare Daniel xii. 9, with Rev. xxii. 10.

keeping one great lesson ever on our mind—viz. "Let your loins be girt about, and your lights burning, and ye yourselves like men that wait for their Lord."*

It now remains that I lay before you a brief outline of the subjects which I purpose treating in these chapters.

I shall not of course profess to speak of *every* subject which may be supposed to come within the range of *unfulfilled Prophecy*. I shall confine myself to those predictions which relate distinctly to the second Advent of the Lord Jesus Christ,—His Kingdom,—and His people's glory; noting those points more especially which call upon the servants of the Lord to watch and pray.

The GENERAL ORDER of our subjects will be as follows:

1.—THE STATE OF THE WORLD-AND THE CHURCH WHEN THE COMING OF THE LORD DRAWS NEAR.
2.—ISRAEL AND ANTICHRIST.
3.—THE ADVENT.
4.—THE JUDGMENT OF THE NATIONS.
5.—THE REIGN OF PEACE.
6.—THE FINAL OUTBREAK OF EVIL.
7.—THE GENERAL RESURRECTION OF THE WICKED.
8.—THE NEW JERUSALEM.

Now perhaps to some among my Christian Brethren such a catalogue of subjects bearing upon the Second Advent of our Saviour may seem strange. They

* Luke xxii. 35.

have been used to look for a great day of judgment to burst suddenly upon the world; and then, in its brief twelve or four and twenty hours, all things which appertain to earth to be brought quickly to an end: the Heavens to pass away; the elements to melt; the earth to be burned up; the dead to be raised; the living to be changed; the whole innumerable multitude to rise from out of the midst of the tremendous wreck of nature, and to stand above, in heights unknown, before the Son of Man, that they may there and then be judged, and upon each soul a sentence passed for weal or woe! The wicked to go forth accordingly, to the eternal flames of Hell, and every righteous soul be ushered into everlasting happiness.

It will be my endeavor in the course of these chapters to look very carefully into Scripture, upon the subjects which will come before us. I will ask my fellow Christians to bear kindly with me, if my views do not agree with all their pre-conceived ideas, and to follow me from passage to passage of the Word of God with patience, while I deal, as briefly as I can, consistently with clearness, upon these most important matters.

And now, let me entreat those Christian Brethren who are looking with expectant eyes for the appearing of their Lord,—to pray that God may send His Holy Spirit down with quickening power, that many who have hitherto been satisfied with a mere outward show of deference towards the doctrine of the great Advent of our Lord, may look for it with an expectant mind; and coming to the Saviour Jesus, that His all-atoning blood may cleanse, and His unblemished righteousness adorn, their souls; may be found ready when He shall appear, and in eternal joy unite with those who shall lift up the willing voice, and say one to another as they gaze upon His once despised, but now most glorious countenance, "Lo! THIS IS OUR GOD; WE HAVE WAITED FOR HIM, AND HE WILL SAVE US:—THIS IS THE LORD; WE HAVE WAITED FOR HIM, WE WILL BE GLAD AND REJOICE IN HIS SALVATION."

CHAPTER II.

THE WORLD AND THE CHURCH.

"Take heed to yourselves, lest, at any time your hearts be over-charged with surfeiting and drunkenness, and cares of this life, and so that day come upon you unawares. For as a snare shall it come on all them that dwell on the face of the whole earth. Watch ye therefore and pray always, that ye may be accounted worthy to escape all these things that shall come to pass, and to stand before the Son of Man."—LUKE xxi. 34, 36.

IN the former chapter I endeavored to establish the duty of studying the unfulfilled prophecies, and to set forth the manner in which such study should be carried on. I then laid down the general scheme I had in mind; upon which I will now enter without farther preface.

THE CONDITION OF THE WORLD AND THE CHURCH AS THE ADVENT OF OUR LORD APPROACHES will form the subject of the present chapter.

An idea is abroad in Christian society, that through the progress of civilization and the gradual spread of the Gospel, a Millennium of Peace and Righteousness will be introduced, and this world will thereby be prepared for the Second Advent of our Lord. This is, without doubt, a *grand theory*, and one which is sure to obtain favor; but it is FALSE. The Word of God has nowhere sanctioned such a notion: indeed the *direct contrary* is clearly laid before us. Moreover we ourselves are called to live in days when science and civilization have arrived at wondrous height. Men's talents never were so highly tutored: human skill was never so developed: refinement also has attained to exquisite perfection in almost every grade of life. But what of PEACE? It is needful to speak very cautiously respecting it, and to give all our science a direction which concerns the munitions of war. And what of RIGHTEOUSNESS? In every circle of society (clothed indeed in seemly garment, but all the more iniquitous by consequence) *ungodliness abounds: Sin* grows in presumption and comes in with gentleness and plausibility, to take possession and to overthrow. We are not, therefore, making progress towards this visionary excellence. Nay, are we not departing farther day by day, from what is good and holy? I need not surely stay to offer proofs of these positions. They are patent to the most casual observers of the times. No one who mingles with society, or reads the daily newspapers, can help lamenting that the case is *even thus*. It does not *seem*, therefore, as if we were *at present* making progress toward Millennial perfection. No one, I should suppose, can say that matters lead to any such conclusion.

But let us look, now, at our Bibles, and there find what we must expect as times flies on, and the Great Day of Christ approaches.

In the first place, we find that nothing is laid down in plainer terms than this, "Iniquity shall abound" in a peculiar and fearful manner as the time draws near.

Our SAVIOUR'S words are powerful, which in the twenty-fourth chapter of St. Matthew, and elsewhere, foretell some of the wonders of that "end" for which we look. He cheers us indeed by the declaration that, "The Gospel of the Kingdom shall be preached in all the world for a witness unto all nations," and by other gladdening assurances: but then, on the other hand, He forewarns us how that as the end draws near "iniquity shall abound" and "the love of many shall wax cold." He reminds us of the days of NOAH, when the world was totally regardless of the fear of God, when "every imagination of the thoughts of man's heart was only evil continually,"* and tells us "So shall it be also in the days of the Son of Man."† He refers, likewise, to the days of LOT, when men were "sinners before the Lord exceedingly,‡ and declares "Even thus shall it be in the day when the Son of Man is revealed."§ And elsewhere we find the Saviour asking the conclusive question, "Nevertheless, when the Son of Man cometh, shall He find faith on the earth?"‖

But let us see now what the word of the inspired APOSTLES was upon this subject. ST. PAUL deals therewith plainly, in his second Epistle to the Thessalonians: "Let no man deceive you by any means, for that day shall not come, except there come a falling away first, and that Man of Sin be revealed, the Son of Perdition . . . . . whom the Lord shall consume with the Spirit of His mouth, and shall destroy with the brightness of His coming. Even him, whose

---

* Gen. vi. 5. † Luke xvii. 26. ‡ Gen. xiii. 13.
§ Luke xvii. 30. ‖ Luke xviii. 8.

3

coming is after the working of Satan, with all power, and signs, and lying wonders, and with all deceivableness of unrighteousness in them that perish; because they received not the love of the truth, that they might be saved."* So likewise, in his second Epistle to Timothy, we find him speaking of the "perilous times" which shall come "in the last days," when "Men shall be lovers of their own selves, covetous, boasters, proud, blasphemers, disobedient to parents, unthankful, unholy, without natural affection, truce-breakers, false-accusers, incontinent, fierce, despisers of those that are good, traitors, heady, high-minded, lovers of pleasures more than lovers of God; having a form of godliness, but denying the power thereof."† St. Jude, also, in his short Epistle, warns us how that in the last time there shall be "mockers" who shall walk "after their own ungodly lusts."‡ To the same conclusion does the book of Revelation lead us.§

But if the evidence be so strong in the *New* Testament, we may expect to find some intimation of the same thing in the *Old* Testament also; since that part of the Word of God dwells likewise very fully on the subject of the Second Advent.

On reference, we shall find that the *Old* Testament writers had *by no means* been permitted to lose sight of it. When Isaiah speaks so strongly of the final judgments which shall come upon the earth, *making it empty—laying it waste, turning it upside down—defiling it under the inhabitants thereof;*—what is the great cause assigned but that men *"have transgressed*

* 2 Thess. ii. 3—10. † 2 Timothy iii. 1—5.
‡ Jude xviii. § Rev. xvi., xvii., xix., &c.

the laws, changed the ordinances, broken the everlast-
ing covenant!" "*Therefore,*" (it is added) "hath
the curse devoured the earth, ... fear, and the
pit, and the snare, are upon its inhabitants," it shall
"be moved exceedingly,"—reel to and fro like a
drunkard, and be removed, like a cottage, and the
transgression thereof shall be heavy upon it."* So
again in speaking of the judgments which shall
accompany the introduction of that day, when the
wolf and the lamb shall feed together and the lion
shall eat straw like the bullock," and when "they
shall not hurt nor destroy;" he says, "Behold the
Lord will come with fire and with His chariots like a
whirlwind, to render His anger with fury, and His
rebuke with flames of fire; for by fire, and by His
sword will the Lord plead with all flesh, and the slain
of the Lord shall be many. . . . . . . *For I know their
works and their thoughts.* It shall come that I will
gather all nations and tongues, and they shall come
and see my glory. . . . . And they shall go forth,
and look upon the *carcases of the men that have
transgressed against* ME: for their worm shall not
die, neither shall their fire be quenched, and they
shall be an abhorring unto all flesh."†

So far for a glance only at the testimony of ISAIAH.
Let me now refer you to the Prophet DANIEL. In
the seventh chapter we have the four great Kingdoms
of the world's history brought before us; the *fourth*
enduring till the day when the judgment shall sit, and
the Saints of the Most High shall take the reins of
government. Now, although *through wickedness,*

* Isaiah xxiv. 6—22. † Isaiah lxvi. 15—24.

each of these Kingdoms was to meet with its destruction, the iniquity of *the fourth only* is dwelt upon, and the sinfulness of this Kingdom it is declared, shall *not abate* until "*the judgment shall be set, and the books opened.*"* Of the last form of this Kingdom's government, it is declared, "He shall speak great words against the Most High, and shall wear out the Saints of the Most High, and think to change times and laws; and they shall be given unto His hand, until a time, and times, and the dividing of time." And then it is added, "But the judgment shall sit, and they shall take away his dominion, to consume, and to destroy it unto the end."† But let me ask you carefully to study the seventh, eighth, ninth, and eleventh chapters of this Prophecy; and you will, I think, see clearly that as the time of the Millennial reign approaches, we are to expect *wickedness to abound, and practise, and prosper*, with a mighty hand.

The glorious rest, therefore, which this world shall enjoy, will not be *gradually developed:* it will not be brought about by education, nor by the preaching of the Gospel; nor by the mutual consent of nations, nor by any instrumentality whatsoever which mankind will bring to bear on its direction. "*The whole world lieth in wickedness.*" It *has* so lain since Adam fell:—It *will* so lie until the day of its regeneration. And as we near that day, the Word will be heard with an increasing power, which says, "Woe to the inhabiters of the earth, and of the sea! for the devil is come down unto you, having great

* Daniel vii. 10.   † Daniel vii. 23—26.

wrath because he knoweth that he hath but a short time."*

But farther. There shall be a PERIOD OF TRIBULATION such as has not been "since the beginning of the world."

Our Saviour foretold "famines, pestilences, and earthquakes,"—"war and rumors of wars"—nation rising against nation, and kingdom against kingdom.†
These were to be "the *beginning* of sorrows," the *precursors* of "THE GREAT TRIBULATION."

I know not how to choose from a mass of Scripture passages which speak of the tremendous trials of the last days; the fit accompaniments of the increasing wickedness. The Lord, as ISAIAH prophesied, "will punish the world for their evil and the wicked for their iniquity." "I will cause (said God) the arrogancy of the proud to cease, and will lay low the haughtiness of the terrible. I will make a man more precious than fine gold; even a man than the golden wedge of Ophir. Therefore, I will shake the heavens; and the earth shall remove out of her place, in the wrath of the Lord of Hosts, and in the day of His fierce anger."‡ "Come near ye nations to hear; and hearken ye people; let the earth hear, and all that is therein; the world, and all things that come forth of it. For the indignation of the Lord is upon all nations, and His fury upon all their armies: He hath utterly destroyed them, He hath delivered them to the slaughter. Their slain also shall be cast out, and their stink shall come up out of their carcases, and the mountains shall be melted with their blood. And

---

* Rev. xii. 12.   † Matt. xxiv. 6—8.   ‡ Isaiah xiii. 11—13.

all the host of heaven shall be dissolved, and the heavens shall be rolled together as a scroll: and all their host shall fall down as the leaf falleth off from the vine and as the falling fig from the fig-tree."* Thus does the Lord speak of a time yet to come, a time fearful with exceeding terror for all nations of the earth, betokening the approach of the great day of God.

But let us refer to JEREMIAH. The words of *his* prophecy are no less terrible in that remarkable twenty-fifth chapter wherein he dwells so strongly upon the judgments of the latter day, when "the Lord shall roar from on high, and utter His voice from His holy habitation," and when He shall "plead with all flesh," and "give them that are wicked to the sword. Behold evil shall go forth from nation to nation, and a great whirlwind shall be raised up from the coasts of the earth. And the slain of the Lord shall be, at that day, from one 'end of the earth even unto the other end of the earth: they shall not be lamented, neither gathered, nor buried: they shall be as dung upon the ground."†

Or, let us hear the testimony of the prophet JOEL, when *he also* foretells important details of the "last days." "Proclaim ye this among the Gentiles; Prepare war, wake up the mighty men, let all the men of war draw near; let them come up; beat your plough-shares into swords, and your pruning-hooks into spears: let the weak say, I am strong. Assemble yourselves, and come all ye heathen, and gather yourselves together round about: thither cause thy mighty ones to

---

* Isaiah xxxiv. 1—4.   † Jeremiah xxv. 32, 33.

come down, O Lord. Let the heathen be awakened, and come up to the valley of Jehoshaphat: for there will I sit to judge all the heathen round about. Put ye in the sickle; for the harvest is ripe: come get you down: for the press is full, the vats overflow: for their wickedness is great. Multitudes, multitudes in the valley of decision." And this shall come to pass as that foretold time approaches, when "The sun and moon shall be darkened, and the stars shall withdraw their shining," and "The Lord shall roar out of Zion, and utter His voice from Jerusalem; and the heavens shall shake; and the Lord will be the hope of His people, and the strength of the children of Israel," and men shall know that the Lord dwelleth in Zion, and Jerusalem shall be holy, and there shall no strangers pass through her any more, but Judah shall dwell for ever, and Jerusalem from generation to generation.*

And so might we quote from Prophet after Prophet. But we have enough to show us, beyond doubt, that when the Lord shall come again upon this earth it will be in the midst of *dreadful carnage: the heathen raging: the people imagining a vain thing: the kings of the earth setting themselves together against the Lord and against His anointed.*† There will be indeed, "a voice of lamentation, and of bitter weeping:" the antitype of Rachel weeping for her children, and refusing to be comforted because they are not:‡ for the wine-press of the wrath of God shall be trodden, and blood will come out thereof

---

* Joel iii. † Psalm ii. 1—2. ‡ Jer. xxxi. 15.

(as it is declared) "Even to the horse-bridles by the space of a thousand and six hundred furlongs."*

But there shall be OTHER CAUSES OF SAD TROUBLE in the last days, besides those which we have now referred to.

Satan, knowing "that he hath but a short time," will grow *desperate.* He will "come down having great wrath."† A peculiar power will be permitted, and he will exercise it wisely. There shall be "fearful sights and great wonders. Blood and fire, and pillars of smoke." "Doctrines of devils" advocated and received. Wandering spirits" communicated with, heeded and trusted.‡ Men energized by Satan and empowered to work miracles upon the earth—of kind without example on the page of history; iniquity and craft performing such astounding deeds "as to deceive, if it were possible, even the elect;"‖ the earth filled full of "trouble and darkness, dimness and anguish;" so that men in their multitudes shall be "*driven to darkness.*"

Thus wickedness and tribulation, terrible and increasing, shall be found among the characteristics of THE WORLD as the great day of the Lord draws near, and there shall not be (as so many vainly think) a

---

* Rev. xiv. 20.   † Rev. xii. 12.

‡ "Now the Spirit speaketh expressly that in the latter days some shall depart from the faith, giving heed to seducing (πλανοις *i. e. wandering*) spirits, and doctrines of *devils speaking lies in hypocrisy.*" 1 Tim. iv. 1, 2. See also Isaiah viii. 19—22, 2 Thess. ii. 3—12, Rev. xiii. 11—16, and xvi. 13, 14. This subject is very faithfully dealt with in a little work by REV. E. NANGLE, M.A., Rector of Skreen, entitled "Spiritualism fairly tried." (Werteim and Macintosh.)

‖ Matt. xxiv. 24.

gradual increase of true enlightenment, righteousness, and peace, to usher in the gentle reign of the Redeemer. For aught then which we learn from the state of things around us in the world, we may be even at the present moment *drawing near* to the great Advent of our God.

But what now as to the CHURCH? This is a point of deepest interest with the Lord's people. The world will always be at work for its own god, and therefore it is no marvel if it reap the fruit of such a servitude: but how the children of the Lord will fare amid the increased wickedness, and in the day of vengeance, is a matter as to which the earnest Christian *must desire* to be informed. The judgments we have spoken of are to be *world-wide*. Exceptions seem to have been made but sparingly on the prophetic page. A man is to be "more precious than the golden wedge of Ophir." "The slain of the Lord" are to be "from one end of the earth to the other." Indeed, "When the Lord cometh *shall he find faith*,"—*shall he find a real Christian*,—"upon the earth?" But how is this to be? Will the Lord's people then deny their faith, consort with the wicked, and be consumed with the transgressors? *O surely not.* The people of the Lord are *many;* multitudes in every nation under heaven. We cannot think they will apostatize. Nay, who shall make so great multitudes afraid? Moreover, the Inspired Word is plain upon the point. *They shall not apostatize.* The iniquity and tribulation shall be such as to deceive even the Elect "if it were possible;" but it is *not possible;* as Christ has said, "MY sheep, hear my voice and I know them, and they follow me, and I give unto them eternal life, *and they shall never perish, neither shall any (man) pluck them out of my hand.*"* Indeed a great change must pass upon the world before the day *can* come wherein the Church of Christ upon the earth, taken as a whole, will be the subject of a persecution unto death. It is true that both Daniel† and St. John‡ speak clearly upon the subject of a last great persecution which is to afflict God's servants; and *that* immediately before the coming of the Lord for judgment. But if we examine what they say as to the state of things which will exist upon the earth, at that period, (as we must presently,) we shall see that the whole aspect of the world's affairs will have undergone A CHANGE, *sudden* and *wonderful, brought about by God himself.*

The *very strongest* intimation which occurs in Scripture about the spread of Gospel faith and the spiritual standing of the Church—its zeal—its devotedness—its love for souls—and its position of power in the world when the great day is near; appears to be that which our Lord Jesus Christ himself gave to his disciples when he said—"This gospel of the kingdom shall be preached in all the world, for a witness unto all nations: and then shall the end come."|| But this says *very little* in the direction of *an universal reception* of the Gospel. The Gospel is but to be *preached* everywhere "for a witness." Not to be *received* everywhere, nor even by *every*

---

* John x. 27, 28.　　　† Daniel vii. 25, and xi. 31—37.
‡ Rev. xx. 4.　　　|| Matt. xxiv. 25.

nation. Nothing more indeed need be done, nothing more need be expected than we find to have already taken place. For anything that is declared in this passage we may expect the Second Advent of our Saviour now. It is MARVELLOUS how *very little* we read in Scripture about the Spiritual standing of the Church of Christ as the Millennial age approaches, and how *much* we read of the abounding wickedness of *the world*, its sinfulness increasing, its evil seducers waxing worse and worse, deceiving and being deceived.

By what is said respecting the amazing growth of wickedness "in the last days," I think we may expect that the true people of the Lord will appear more decidedly distinct, and that they will stand out to greater disadvantage in the eyes of men. Not, however, that mankind will be in the main *without religion.* Very evidently *otherwise. Religiousness* will be a mark of the last days. Men will have "a *form* of godliness, but *deny the power* thereof:" they will be "ever learning, but never able to come to the knowledge of the truth:"* preparing themselves, although they know it not, for the worship of that wicked one,—whose coming shall be "after the power of Satan," and who "as God," sitting in the Temple of God, will show himself "that he *is* God."†

SATISFACTORY, therefore, the state of the *outward* church will *not* be. And the *true spiritual* church of the Lord's believing people will be MUCH TRIED. There will be an urgent call for watchfulness and prayer, that the things which remain and are ready

* 2 Timothy iii. 3—5.   † 2 Thess. ii. 4.

to die may be strengthened;—there will be need for looking well both to the girdle and to the lamp, and for the maintenance of a simple, childlike faith in the all-sufficient Saviour.

But now the minds of some amongst us will perhaps be in a strait, by reason of what seems to be a CONTRADICTION. We have seen that the Church will *not apostatize*—that a *persecution unto death* (so far as the *whole* Church is concerned) will *not take place*,—AND YET that our Lord Himself has intimated, and the Inspired Writers have led us clearly to conclude, that when the judge of all men shall descend upon the earth, it will be—as it were—*a question whether He will find* ONE TRUE BELIEVER THERE; *whether there will be* ANY CHURCH WHATEVER *in the world to welcome His appearing.* In other words,—that there *will be* a people, *ready, waiting, watching,* for the Lord's Advent; and yet that there will be *no faith, no love, no readiness,* and *no expectancy;* but only *sin, misery,* and *anguish of heart,* among the multitudes of earth.

But there is NO REAL CONTRADICTION here;—all is plain and clear: although the solution of the difficulty may perchance oppose itself to the pre-conceived ideas of many Christian people. Let us now, however, proceed to an examination of this matter.

We will again refer to our Lord's assertion, "As the days of Noe were, so shall the coming of the Son of Man be. . . . As it was in the days of Lot . . . even thus shall it be in the day when the Son of Man is revealed."*

* Luke xvii. 26—30, and elsewhere.

Now NOAH was safely shut up in the Ark—"God shut him in"* *before* the flood descended upon the earth. And LOT was lodged in the little city ZOAR, which was given as an answer to his prayers,—*before* the fire and brimstone were poured down on Sodom. We remember how the destroying angel bade him quickly leave the doomed city—Haste thee, escape thither, (that is to Zoar,) *for I cannot do anything till thou be come thither.*"† SO THEN IT SHALL BE WHEN THE SON OF MAN IS REVEALED: the waiting people of the Lord *shall be delivered:* they shall be taken to a *place of safety* ere the fearful burden of the last great tribulation shall descend upon the earth's inhabitants.

But let us take some further evidence upon this point. In the text which forms the heading of this chapter, we find our Saviour forewarning his disciples —"Take heed, lest at any time your hearts be overcharged with surfeiting, and drunkenness, and cares of this life, and so that day *come upon you unawares. For as a snare shall it come* ON ALL THEM THAT DWELL ON THE FACE OF THE WHOLE EARTH. Watch ye, therefore, and pray always, that ye may be accounted *worthy to* ESCAPE *all those things that shall come to pass, and to stand before the Son of Man.*" Surely this makes matters very plain. The day of Christ shall come "*unawares*" upon "*all* them that dwell on the face of the *whole earth.*" NONE shall be prepared for it. But it is *not thus* to come upon the *waiting servants* of the Lord. They will be accounted worthy to escape—(ἐκφυγεῖν to flee out of) all those terrors which the people of the world must suffer,—"The distress of nations,"—"the perplexity"—"the fear" which shall make men's hearts to fail—and the shaking of the powers of heaven. They shall but "see these things *begin* to come to pass," and then they shall be called away, and "*Stand before the Son of Man.*"*

But we will examine this important matter further yet. St. PAUL has a word upon it in his first Epistle to the Thessalonians, which reads as follows: "If we believe that Jesus died and rose again, even so them *also* which sleep in Jesus will God bring with Him."† "Them ALSO!"—who then *besides* them shall form a portion of his train? The Apostle tells us—"For this we say unto you by the word of the Lord, that we which are alive and remain until the coming of the Lord, shall *not prevent* (that is "go before" or "be in advance of") them which are asleep. For the Lord Himself shall descend from heaven with a shout, with the voice of the Archangel and with the trump of God; and the *dead in Christ shall rise* FIRST. THEN *we which are alive and remain* shall be caught up together with them in *the clouds to meet the Lord in the air.*"‡ Let us observe the order:—the *dead* in Christ FIRST, and THEN the *living* in Christ, are to go and "MEET the Lord IN THE AIR," as He descends from above; that He may "*bring*" them "*with Him*" to the earth, among that glorious train which then shall do Him honor. Thus far is the testimony of the Apostle Paul clear. He does not indeed tell us what shall

* Luke xxi. 34—36.　　† 1 Thess. iv. 14.　　‡ 1 Thess. iv. 15—17.

take place in the world after the living in Christ shall be changed, and safely taken to the presence of their Lord; but, so far as his testimony goes, it is very decided in support of the doctrine which we have advanced. And if we take the word of Paul in connection with that of our Lord which we have quoted, we shall find it perfectly evident that the Lord's people who shall be living upon the earth at the time of our Saviour's coming will be caught up to meet Him in the air, and will abide with Him in safety till the period of the tribulation shall be over.

But let us strengthen our position, by examining what the PROPHETS OF THE OLD TESTAMENT have advanced.

We will turn first to ISAIAH. We find he has devoted the twenty-fifth and twenty-sixth chapters of his prophecy to the subject now before us. He speaks of a day wherein the Lord will "swallow up death in victory," "wipe away tears from off all faces," and "take away the rebuke of his people from off all the earth;" a day wherein it shall be said, "Lo! this is our God: we have waited for Him, and He will save us;" a day wherein the Lord "will keep him in perfect peace whose mind is stayed on Him;" a day wherein the *Lord's hand shall be lifted up, and though the wicked "will not see, they shall see."* Now we find a wonderful word spoken by the Prophet, both concerning these *wicked ones who* "will not see," and the *people who have waited for the Lord.* Of the wicked he declares, "They are dead, they *shall not live:* they are deceased, they *shall not rise:* therefore, Thou hast visited and destroyed them, and made all their memory to perish."* And then after an expression of wonder and gratitude to God for the increase and prosperity of *Israel,* which shall take place at that time, he continues, (still addressing God,) "*Thy* dead *shall* live, together with my dead body shall they arise." And then (as it were) turning to *the people of the Lord, who shall be lying in the silent tomb,* he adds— "Awake and sing, ye that dwell in the dust: for thy dew is as the dew of herbs, and the earth shall cast out the dead." And then again addressing *others,* he says—"Come my people, enter thou into thy chambers, and shut thy doors about thee: hide thyself, as it were, for a little moment, until the indignation be overpast. For, behold, the Lord cometh out of His place to punish the inhabitants of the earth for their iniquity: the earth also shall disclose her blood, and shall no more cover her slain." This last address could not certainly have been intended *for the dead.* They,—already secure against the sword,—would be beyond the reach of comfort from such exhortation: a punishment designed for the "inhabitants of the earth," a punishment, concerning the effect of which it is declared—"The earth shall disclose her *blood,* and shall no more cover her SLAIN"—could not be profitable for men *already dead.* The LIVING surely must be addressed here. THE LIVING PEOPLE OF THE LORD. Those "who are alive and remain" unto His coming. Such (speaking after the manner of men) would be unsafe amid the fearful tribulation to be poured out upon the unbe-

* Isaiah xxvi. 14.

lieving world. Therefore, they are *called away*
BEFORE "The Lord cometh out of His place to
punish the inhabitants of the earth for their iniquity."

But let us take the word of yet another Prophet,—
DANIEL. We will refer to the twelfth chapter of his
prophecy. The chapter opens thus—"And at that
time shall Michael stand up, the great prince which
standeth for the children of Thy people; and there
shall be a time of trouble, such as never was since
there was a nation, even to that same time: and *at
that time Thy people shall be delivered, every one that
shall be found written in the book.* And *many* of
them that sleep in the dust of the earth shall awake,
some to everlasting life, and some to shame and everlasting contempt."[*] Now this passage requires a
little explanation. It appears that at the time when
the great Prince shall stand up, there shall be AN UN-
PRECEDENTED TRIBULATION, but every one whose
name "shall be found written in *the book*" shall
be delivered: he shall not be a sufferer: he shall
(as we have seen elsewhere) arise to meet the Lord,
and abide with him in safety. Moreover, "*many* of
them that sleep in the dust of the earth shall awake."
"*Many*"—NOT ALL,—*a part only* of the dead. But
who of these? The passage tells us, as it continues,
"Some to everlasting life, and some to shame and
everlasting contempt." But here we must remove a
difficulty. I believe there is an acknowledged incor-
rectness in rendering the Hebrew words which are
translated SOME. They should be "*these*" and

* Daniel xii. 1, 2.

4

"*those.*"* With this alteration the passage will read thus, "Many of them that sleep in the dust of the earth shall awake, THESE (who awake) to *everlasting life*, and *those* (who still sleep on in death, are reserved) *to shame and everlasting contempt.*"

In Daniel's prophecy, therefore, we find the same important doctrine. The *living Saints* shall be changed, and delivered from the tribulation: the *departed Saints* shall be raised and enter into everlasting life. The *wicked among the living* shall be left to go through the time of trouble; the *wicked among the departed*, shall be reserved for a *future* resurrection day, when they shall arise "to shame and everlasting contempt."

But now that we may finally establish the fact before us, let us turn attention for a moment to an allegory which occurs in the Book of Revelation, where the approach of the end of this dispensation is referred to under the vision of "the seventh Trumpet."† The Church of Christ is brought before us under the figure of A WOMAN CLOTHED WITH THE SUN, whose *child* about to to be born, is anxiously waited for by *the Dragon:* but as soon as he is brought forth, *God interferes on his behalf, and he is caught up to Heaven.* This done, the persecution commences against the woman, and continues for a thousand two hundred and three-score days. This persecution is accompanied by a word of woe to the inhabitants of the earth and

---

* ראֵלֶּה .... אֵלֶּה in Hebrew are the same as—hi et illi—in Latin, viz: "these and these, or these and those;" as indeed we find the same words translated in Isaiah xlix. 12, "Behold *these* shall come from far, and *these* from the coast of Sinim."

† Revelation xii.

of the sea, for that the devil is come down to them, having great wrath, because he knoweth he hath but a short time. Now this allegory speaks for itself. I have assumed that the woman *represents* the church of Christ. This cannot be assuming too much. There is no room, I think, for doubt concerning it. But *if this be granted* the details scarcely need a word of explanation. The man-child is the *first-fruits;* a certain completed number of the Lord's elect. The Church immediately before the *great tribulation*, gives forth this, her first-born, to the hand of God, who straightway takes it to Himself.

All then is clear so far, and we may conclude with certainty, that when the day of trouble is about to dawn upon the world *every one* among God's waiting people—*every sincere believer in the Lord Jesus*, be he living on the earth or buried in the grave, shall rise to meet that Great Redeemer in the air, and shall be safe with Him above, until the time arrive when He, with all His saints, shall come to execute His fearful judgments on the earth's inhabitants.

But let us pause a moment to reflect about *ourselves*. If the trumpet of the Lord should sound this day for the departure of the Saints of Christ, *should we be ready?* It is written, "In that *day*, even in that *night*, (for the call will reach to every place upon the surface of our globe, where it is *day* and where it is *night*) "two men shall be in the one bed, one shall be taken and the other left: two women shall be grinding together, one shall be taken and the other left." Which then would it be in our case? TAKEN or LEFT? O, if we are putting off the things of our eternity to a future day, we should be LEFT. If we have not gone as helpless sinners to the Lord Jesus Christ, that we might obtain pardon through His blood, we should be LEFT. But if we have through grace, with all our hearts sought the Redeemer; laid our sins on Him by faith; received Him as our Lord and Saviour in sincerity and truth, then we should be TAKEN:—taken up to meet our King, and be with Him for ever. O, surely this is not a time for luke-warmness, fer deferring things of everlasting moment to a future day, but for the most earnest *circumspection, watchfulness, prayer,* and *zeal.* O, let us see,—each one for himself,—that we are not found wanting in the sight of the Great Judge of all.

But we have not yet quite dwelt sufficiently upon the state of our Redeemer's Church. The woman in the Apocalyptic allegory fled into the wilderness and remained there for three years and a half, nourished and protected by God, AFTER her man-child had been caught up. There shall be, therefore, even while the tribulation lasts, A TRUE AND FAITHFUL CHURCH: per-secuted, but not forsaken; for we read that "the ser-pent cast out of his mouth water as a flood that he might cause the woman to be carried away thereby; and that the dragon was wroth with the woman, and went to make war with the remnant of her seed which keep the commandments of God, and have the testi-mony of Jesus Christ." But this allegorical evidence of a Church existing and persecuted, *after the first-fruits have been removed,* is corroborated by another passage more clear and free from allegory in the twentieth chapter. Here we find St. John when speaking of the introduction of the Millennial reign, making reference to certain, who should suffer martyrdom under "*the Beast,*" (which is the name given to the Antichrist in the Book of Revelation). Martyrs therefore who are to suffer death *after the first-fruits of the earth shall have departed.* "And I saw thrones and they sat upon them, and judgment was given unto them. And I saw the souls of them that were beheaded for the witness of Jesus and for the Word of God, and *which had not worshipped the Beast,* neither his image, neither had received his mark in their foreheads or in their hands; and they lived and reigned with Christ a thousand years."*

Thus it is evident, that *after* the departure of the first-fruits; *after* the man-child shall be caught up to Heaven; *after* the Lord's waiting people shall be taken away to meet their Saviour in the air,—there shall be found a CHURCH—a people serving Christ in truth,—and against these a persecution shall be effectually directed, even unto death.

But let us see how this *can be,* for there is a great difficulty here. *Every believer will have gone. A vast multitude out of every nation under Heaven will have been taken hence.* The Lord will have descended into the heights above the world; *invisibly, perhaps, to all except His people;*—I say, INVISIBLY TO ALL EXCEPT HIS PEOPLE;—for I think there is no warrant given us in Holy Scripture for asserting that there shall be *any token* granted to the unconverted world *before the tribulation,* to warn them of the descent of Jesus into the air to call His saints. The unbelievers

* Revelation xx. 4.

will not—I think—hear a trumpet-sound, nor will they see a lightning flash. They will, indeed, be witnesses of these things, "*immediately after* the tribulation of those days," as the twenty-fourth chapter of St. Matthew testifies: but *not before* the tribulation. Probably the dead in Christ will be raised *silently* and *invisibly*, before suspicion is excited amongst men,—no sod upturned: no grave disturbed: only the body gone; and *so*, perchance, it may be missed. Then as suddenly the removal of the *living* people of the Lord, will follow. In *silence* also, and *without a sign* afforded to the unbelieving world, (for anything that has appeared in Scripture to the contrary.) They will be taken hence,—drawn up at once to Christ. So they too will be missed and sought for upon earth, but nowhere found. In every neighborhood will be the cry for them. In house after house will be a bitter wailing raised because of them. O, what a day of sadness and of terror will that be! What dread will sit on every countenance! for thus shall the world be in one moment stripped of all the pure, and just, and holy who adorned its surface, and be left a WICKED WORLD INDEED.

But what may we expect will *follow* if the day of grace be not for ever at that moment closed? Most certainly A GREAT REVIVAL OF RELIGION. For imagine the sensation which must be produced among the unconverted masses by the sudden removal of each Christian from the surface of the whole earth. *One, two, three,* out of every family *gone*—no man can tell where—passed from sight in the twinkling of an eye!! Two in a bed; *one taken!* two at a mill;

one taken! two friends conversing; *one taken!* two men transacting business; *one taken!* Husband and wife, brother and sister, master and servant; *one taken!* Will not men begin to think? Will not many scoffers fall upon their knees and pray? Will not the Bible be searched for with new eyes? Will not men's hearts fail them for fear and for looking after those things which are coming upon the earth? O, methinks there will be a stirring up of lukewarm ministers in that day; a crowding into churches such as never has been witnessed. A *change, indeed,* will come over all the face of earth's society. And so indeed we find—when this matter is dealt with in the fourteenth chapter of the Revelation—that *immediately* the first-fruits unto God and the Lamb, are spoken of as being with the Lord above, *an angel* flies in the midst of Heaven, "having the everlasting Gospel to preach to them that dwell on the earth, and to every nation, and kindred, and tongue, and people, saying with a loud voice, Fear God, and give glory to Him, for the hour of His judgment is come."* But clearly, though there may be many who will truly turn to God in that day, yet the Devil will find means to blind the masses of the world to the true state of things; for as we pursue the chapter we perceive that after Babylon is fallen, which is the next event that will transpire, and Antichrist is established upon his throne, "*the patience of the saints*" is brought before us; and it is added—"Blessed are the dead which die in the Lord from henceforth."† And immediately takes place the HARVEST OF THE

* Revelation xiv. 6, 7. † Revelation xiv. 13.

EARTH, which seems to be a second gathering together of God's people unto Him,—perhaps through the medium of a fearful burst of persecution, which shall clear the earth of all who shall refuse the mark and worship of the Beast,—and so the number of the Lord's Elect will be complete, and the way be rendered clear for the tremendous VINTAGE OF THE WRATH OF GOD.*

So far then,—guided by the simple word of Holy Scripture—have we been able to obtain some most important intimations of THE STATE IN WHICH THE WORLD AND THE CHURCH WILL BE FOUND when the Advent of the Lord draws near.

I ask you not to take these things for granted, either that they *are* or *are not* as I have placed them now before you. But I beg of you, as persons *deeply interested* in those most momentous matters, which are—sooner or later—coming upon the earth, to search the Bible *without prejudice*, and without reference to *pre-conceived ideas*, and see for yourselves accurately how these matters stand. And then, as you value your immortal souls, look well to your own state with God. Are you in Christ? Are you forgiven? Are you saved? O what is your condition *now* before the King of Kings? I would urge upon you, *settle these important questions.* See that you are *Christ's indeed:* that you *believe in Him:* and are *alive* through his atoning blood and justifying righteousness,—alive to God,—the children of His grace and love. And then if the glad summons

* Revelation xiv. 20.

should go forth from the high throne of Heaven— "COME UP HITHER,"—you will obey with joy— leave earthly things, as dross, uncared for more,— and depart hence, arrayed in glory, meet for those who sit with the Eternal King upon the Throne of His dominion.

CHAPTER III.

ISRAEL AND ANTICHRIST.

"If another shall come in his own name, him ye will receive."
JOHN v. 43.

HAVING shown, I hope distinctly, that as the day of Christ approaches, the WORLD will display *growth in wickedness;* and the Church will be *removed,*—the *first-fruits* by the call from Heaven, and the *remainder of the harvest* by the hand of persecution;—the minds of many students of the Bible will inquire, "But what is to be the state of THAT PECULIAR PEOPLE WITH WHOM AS A NATION, GOD HAS ENTERED INTO SO RE-MARKABLE A COVENANT?

To the NATION OF ISRAEL and to *him* with whom that nation in the latter days will have a marvellous connection,—even ANTICHRIST,—I shall devote this chapter.

Four thousand years have nearly passed away since the Almighty said to Abraham,—"I will make of thee a great nation . . . . . and in thee shall all the families of the earth be blessed."* Not long after this preliminary promise had been made, the Patriarch was called upon to lift his eyes, and look from the place where he was standing, northward, southward, eastward, and westward; and God said unto him—

* Genesis xii. 1—3.

"All the land which thou seest, to thee I will give it, and to thy seed for ever."* And, on another occasion, very expressly, "Unto thy seed have I given this land, from the river of Egypt unto the great river, the river Euphrates."† This promise is laid down still *more* clearly in the BOOK OF EXODUS, where God declared to Israel,—"I will set thy bounds from the *Red Sea* even unto the *Sea of the Philistines*, and from the *Desert* unto the River.‡ And so again, in DEUTERONOMY,—"Every place whereon the soles of your feet shall tread shall be yours, from the *Wilderness and Lebanon*, from the River, *the River Euphrates*, even unto the *Uttermost Sea* shall your coast be."§ The extent of this promise seems to me to cover THE WHOLE VAST PENINSULA OF ARABIA.‖ Indeed, I think, a careful perusal of the limits of the land of Israel (*as they shall be*) which are given in the forty-seventh chapter of EZEKIEL will show, with something which approaches clearness, that this shall be the true extent of Israel's territory. But be it as it may; the promises of God to Israel in their obvious meaning have reference to an *actual* and *perpetual* POSSESSION of the land. Now the time has NOT YET BEEN when the Children of Israel enjoyed an *actual*

---

* Genesis xiii. 14, 15.   † Genesis xv. 18.

‡ Exodus xxiii. 31.   § Deut. xi. 24.

‖ Rule a line from the northern point of the District of *Lebanon* to the southern point of that of *Sinai*, and draw a perpendicular to it. You will then find that the SEA OF OMAN is "*the Uttermost Sea*." And again,—start from the River Euphrates and draw a perpendicular from the average line of its course, and the RED SEA is "*the Uttermost Sea*." Thus the whole peninsula of Arabia will be included.

possession even from the Euphrates to the Mediterranean; except perhaps for a brief period during the
days of Solomon, of whom it is said, "he reigned over
all the kings from the river even unto the land of the
Philistines and to the border of Egypt;"* but even in
that prosperous day we do not read that Israel enjoyed such *full possession* of the whole, as the promises would lead us to expect.   Moreover, the
strongest and most enlarged predictions as to Israel's
inheritance, have reference to a period which shall
have its dawn when the twelve tribes, dispersed
among the nations, shall have been gathered, and
"the times of the Gentiles be fulfilled."

But we will establish this position by reference to
a few passages from the PROPHETS, passages which
certainly forbid—if any language can forbid—a construction which is not *strictly literal.*   Hear now
first what is written by ISAIAH—"It shall come to
pass in that day, that the Lord shall set his hand
again the *second time* to recover the remnant of His
people, which shall be left from Assyria, and from
Egypt, and from Pathros, and from Cush, and from
Elam, and from Shinar, and from Hamath, and from
the Islands of the Sea.   And he shall set up an
ensign for the nations, and *shall assemble the outcasts
of Israel, and gather the dispersed of Judah from the
four corners of the earth.*"†—But what is *that day*
here referred to as the period when this *second re-
covery* shall take place?   Certainly it is *not* a day
which has yet dawned upon the sons of men, for in
that day "the wolf shall dwell with the lamb; and

---

* 2 Chron. ix. 26.   † Isaiah xi.   See also xviii.—xxiii.—li.

the leopard shall lie down with the kid; and the calf and the young lion and the fatling together, and a little child shall lead them. ...... And the earth shall be full of the knowledge of the Lord, as the waters cover the sea." Take also a proof from JERE-MIAH—"Hear the word of the Lord, O ye nations, and declare it in the isles afar off, and say, He that scattered Israel *will gather him* and keep him as a shepherd doth his flock; for the Lord hath redeemed Jacob, and ransomed him from the hand of him that was stronger than he. *Therefore, they shall come and sing in the heights of Zion, and shall flow together to the goodness of the Lord,* for wheat and for wine, and for oil, and for the young of the flock and of the herd: and their soul shall be as a watered garden, and *they shall not sorrow any more at all.*"* Surely Israel has never thus been gathered hitherto. Her tribes still sorrow as they have been wont to sorrow for so many centuries. This gathering, therefore, must be *future.* But let us take further testimony. We will refer to EZEKIEL. From the *thirty-sixth* chapter to the *end* of the prophecy we find *this subject only* brought before us. It occupies thirteen chapters. In the course of these we cannot fail to note the unmistakable language which the Lord uses —"*I will take you from among the heathen, and gather you out of all countries, and will bring you unto your own land.* Then will I sprinkle clean water upon you, and ye shall be clean. .... A new heart also will I give you, and ye *shall dwell in the land that I gave to your fathers;* and ye shall be

* Jeremiah xxxi. 10—12—37—40; xxiii. 7—26.

my people and I will be your God."* ...... Behold, O my people, I will open your graves and cause
you to come up out of your graves, and *bring you
into the land of Israel* †　Behold I will *take the
children of Israel from among the heathen, whither
they be gone, and will gather them on every side, and
bring them into their own land.*　And I will make
them *one nation* in the land upon the mountains of
Israel; and one king shall be king to them all; and
they shall be *no more two nations*, neither shall they
be divided into two kingdoms any more at all. ......
Moreover, I will make a covenant of peace with them;
it shall be an everlasting covenant with them; and I
will place them, and multiply them, and will set my
sanctuary in the midst of them for evermore."‡

No one surely can pretend to say that these predictions have received accomplishment.　But the
WORD OF GOD IS TRUE, and Israel's day for restoration WILL arrive.

Now we might refer to other passages in EZEKIEL,
or quote from HOSEA,§ JOEL,‖ AMOS,¶ MICAH**, ZE-
PHANIAH,†† ZECHARIAH, or MALACHI.　The two last
mentioned prophesied *after the return from Babylon*,
wherefore their testimony is peculiarly conclusive.
Let us dwell an instant on their words.

ZECHARIAH says, "I will strengthen the house of
Judah and I will save the house of Joseph, and I will
bring them again to place them, for I will have mercy

---

* Ezekiel xxxvi 24—28.　　† Ezekiel xxxvii. 12—14.
‡ Ezekiel xxxvii. 21—28.　　§ Hosea iii. 4—5.
‖ Joel iii. 16, 17.　　¶ Amos ix. 11—15.
** Micah iii. 12, iv. 1, 2.　　†† Zephaniah iii. 14—20.

upon them, and *they shall be as though I had not cast them off.* ...... They shall remember me in far countries, and they shall live with their children, and *turn again.* I will *bring them again also out of the land of Egypt, and gather them out of Assyria, and I will bring them again into the land of Gilead and Lebanon."* "In that day will I make the Governors of Judah like an hearth of fire among the wood. .... And Jerusalem shall be *inhabited again in her own place, even in Jerusalem.* The Lord also shall save the tents of *Judah first.* ..... In that day there shall be a fountain opened to the house of David, and to the inhabitants of Jerusalem, for sin, and for unclean-ness. ...... And men shall dwell in it (Jerusalem) and there shall be *no more utter destruction; but Jerusalem shall be safely inhabited.* In that day shall there be upon the bells of the horses, HOLINESS UNTO THE LORD. ...... Yea every pot in Jerusalem and in Judah shall be holiness unto the Lord of Hosts."† What language can be plainer? Where can room be found for a mere spiritual interpretation?

From MALACHI; the last of the Prophets, we take our final passage,—written, as it was, one hundred years after the return from Babylon,—"I will rebuke the the devourer for your sakes. ...... *All nations shall call you blessed; for ye shall be a delightsome land,* saith the Lord of Hosts."‡

As to the NEW TESTAMENT witness we need not speak at length. But few passages therein have reference to Israel's restoration; still quite enough is

---

* Zechariah xii. 6, 7. † Zechariah xiii. xiv. ‡ Malachi iii. 11, 12.

said to show that the abundant testimony of the Prophets must be *recognized*.

OUR LORD declares "Jerusalem shall be trodden down of the Gentiles, *until the times of the Gentiles be fulfilled;*"* which of course implies that Jerusalem shall be, *after that, no longer trodden down.* Concerning CHRIST it is declared, "The Lord God shall give unto Him the *throne of His father David, and He shall reign over the house of Jacob for ever,* and of His kingdom there shall be *no end.*"† But how is this to be, except a restoration of Israel shall take place? Again; the first sermon preached by an Apostle testifies that David, "being a prophet," knew "that God had sworn with an oath to him, that of the fruit of his loins, *according to the flesh,* he would raise up Christ *to sit on his throne.*"‡ And in the second Apostolic sermon, we read thus, "Repent ye therefore, and be converted, that your sins may be blotted out, when *the times of refreshing* shall come from the presence of the Lord, and *He shall send Jesus Christ,* which before was preached unto you; whom the heavens must receive *until the restitution of all things,* which God hath spoken by the mouth of all His Holy Prophets since the world began."§ Then there *shall* be a "time of refreshing" and "RESTITUTION OF ALL THINGS" when the Lord Jesus Christ shall come from Heaven: and having come, shall sit upon the throne of David. So did the Apostle PETER testify. But let us hear the word of PAUL upon this subject. No less than *three chapters*||

---

* Luke xxi. 24.   † Luke i. 33.   ‡ Acts ii. 30.
§ Acts iii. 19—21. || Rom. ix., x., xi.

of his Epistle to the Romans dwell upon the Lord's
dealings with Israel and the Gentiles, and show
clearly that the many prophecies which went before
upon this point *have not received accomplishment.*
"Hath God cast away His people?" he asks. "God
forbid" is the reply, ... "I would not, brethren,
that ye should be ignorant of this mystery ....
that blindness in part has happened to Israel, *until
the fulness of the Gentiles be come in.* And so *all
Israel* shall be saved: as it is written, There shall
come out of Zion the Deliverer, and shall turn away
ungodliness from Jacob; for this is my covenant unto
them when I shall take away their sins."*

We find evidence enough, then to prove clearly
both from the Old Testament and the New, THAT A
DAY OF RESTORATION IS IN STORE FOR ISRAEL; THAT
HER TRIBES WILL BE GATHERED AND BROUGHT TO
THEIR OWN LAND, and there be placed in a position of
greater blessedness than they have ever yet enjoyed.

Let us then inquire respecting Israel, seeing they
have been so long time scattered over all the earth
WHAT THEIR POSITION IS AT PRESENT; whether there
are *any signs of their return to Palestine;* and
generally *how the Lord is dealing with them.*

As of old time, so we see them *still*—without a
country, without a city, without a temple, dispersed
among the nations, yet *distinct from all.* In Europe,
Asia, Africa, and America the Jew is to be found; a
marked man; important, yet despised; honorable,
yet a by-word and a reproach. The Israelitish people
dwell *alone* though they are *everywhere,* and are not

---

* See also Galatians iii., Hebrews xii., Rev. vii.

reckoned among the nations.* "The precious sons of Zion, comparable to fine gold, how are they esteemed as earthen pitchers, the work of the hands of the potter!"† In some respects however a great change has come over the whole Jewish people. There are signs of life, of nobility, of an effort on behalf of their nationality, which has not for eighteen hundred years existed. Though still *distinct as ever from the rest of men*—the Lord is leading them, from their degraded state *to fill the highest posts of public confidence.* "The number of civic functionaries in FRANCE belonging to the Jewish Communion, is *immensely larger* than the proportionate Israelitish population. M. Achille Fould, at Paris, is but the head of a cohort of Jewish notabilities, financiers, and employés, who are quite as numerous in the departments as in the Capital. At Lyons, Marseilles, and other towns of the South, a large number of the higher government officials are Jews, and at Epinal, the chief city of the department of the Vosges, there is the curious spectacle of the four most eminent civic functionaries,—the paymaster, the military superintendent, the president of the court of justice, and the keeper general of forests, being *Jews, one and all.* Scarcely a century ago, the Jews were hunted like mad dogs in the dominion of the Kaiser, at the mercy of every monk or police officer, and without the slightest security for life and property. Now, in this year, 1862, *two eloquent Jews are the leaders of the great liberal party of the Austrian Reichsrath, and Emperor and Imperial Ministers tremble before the*

---

* Numbers xxiii. 9.   † Lamentations iv. 2.

names of Giskra and Kuranda. More marked than *[*
even in Austria is the rise of the Jews in PRUSSIA.
In the present political agitation, *Hebrew leaders* play
the most conspicuous part, and their participation in
the recent elections was so pronounced that the *Kreuz
Zeitung* for weeks did scarce anything else but abuse
the, so-styled, Jew democrats. According to this
paper, nearly one-fourth the number of *Wäller* chosen
by the people of Prussia to elect the deputies was
composed of Jews. A number about *twenty times as
large as is warranted by the population of the kingdom.*
At Berlin and other large towns the Hebrew prepon-
derance was *still more conspicuous;* and in some of
the ancient POLISH provinces *the descendants of
Abraham had it all their own way.* On classifying
the students of the Universities and high-schools, the
startling result is displayed that the superior aca-
demies are attended by *five times as many Jews in
proportion to Christians,* regard, of course, being had
to the general population, of which the Israelites form
scarcely one and a half per cent. The educated
Jews form part in all the revolutionary movements
from the *Ural* to the *Atlantic,* and from *Lapland* to
Sicily. They are, as it were, the *yeast of the
European fermentation.* The Jew-element is per-
ceptible in the *Galician peasantry,* in the *Finnish
malcontents,* in the *Servia progressists,* and in the
surging masses of *Revolutionary Poland.*"* Moreover, it is confidently stated that wheresoever *of late*
the Jew is found, whether in Scandinavia, in Conti-
nental Europe, in England, on the edge of the North

* Prophetical Journal, October, 1862.

African sea shore, or in the desert of the South,—he has lost the downcast hopelessness of former years; a change has come over him; he feels his membership with a nation which is rising into greatness; his face is looking towards Jerusalem, and he expects with confidence that the day is close at hand when he shall return to the land of the covenant, and inherit the fruition of the promises.

Besides this, *all is getting ready for the reception of Israel in the* HOLY LAND. There is *wealth* there. *Cultivation* is going on, and fruitfulness follows. JERUSALEM itself has undergone a change. The city but a few years since was "poor and miserable in its appearance, the houses mean and dirty, the streets narrow and crooked. *Now* the streets are wide and straight, and alive with the busy hum of traffic. Many handsome buildings have been erected, with beautiful gardens attached, in which flourish all the luscious fruits of this favored clime. Fine churches, synagogues, hospitals, dispensaries, hotels, and stores are everywhere met with, and rich men from Constantinople, Babylon, Bagdad, Damascus, Egypt, England, France, and other places have contributed by their presence to improve and beautify Jerusalem."* Preparation then is going on in Israel's ancient capital; and seeing it is evident that the heart of all the nation is set earnestly upon the hallowed territory, and that the people are obtaining *power in the world and favor also,* of no ordinary kind; I know not what now hinders but that we may seriously expect the sons of Israel will speedily

* Taunton's "Days in which we live."

call Palestine their own, and people that long-pro- ✓
mised land with those WHOSE RIGHT IT IS.

But now a most important question comes before
us: viz., IN WHAT STATE AS TO RELIGION *will the
tribes of Israel be when they return to Palestine?*
Will they *first embrace the Gospel?* or will they be
restored *in unbelief?*

We find the Lord thus speaking by EZEKIEL.
"Because ye are all become dross; behold I will
gather you into the midst of Jerusalem. As they
gather silver, and brass and iron, and lead, and tin,
into the midst of the furnace to blow the fire upon
it, to melt it, so will I gather you *in mine anger and
in my fury, and I will* LEAVE YOU THERE AND MELT
YOU. Yea, I will *gather* you, and *blow* upon you in
the fire of my wrath, and ye *shall be melted in the
midst thereof:* as silver is melted in the midst of the
furnace, so shall ye be melted in the midst thereof:
and ye shall know that I THE LORD *have poured out
my fury upon you.*" Now this gathering of Israel
was to be *after* they should have been scattered
among the heathen, and dispersed in the countries,
and *after* they should have been so dealt with that
the heart of the nation could not "endure" nor the
hands thereof be "strong."* This language is not
certainly consistent with the return of Israel in a
converted state; neither indeed is that of any other
part of Scripture. But rather the whole voice of
prophecy bids us *first* behold the tribes of Israel
(or at least *part thereof*) gathered and established in
the land of their fathers, and then *afterwards,* the

* Ezekiel xxii.

spirit of the Lord outpoured upon their sin-bound
hearts. But I will not dwell further upon this interesting question at the present point of the chapter,
because it will necessarily come before us again as
we proceed.

But now another subject for inquiry of no slight
importance comes before us with regard to Israel's
return. WHO SHALL BE THEIR LEADER? UNDER
WHOSE AUSPICES WILL THEIR RETURN TO PALESTINE
BE BROUGHT ABOUT? BY WHOM WILL THE LAND OF
THE COVENANT BE PLACED IN THEIR POSSESSION?
WHAT POTENTATE WILL INTEREST HIMSELF IN THEIR
RESTORATION, AND TAKE THEIR CASE IN HAND?

We have the answer ready—ANTICHRIST.
The ANTICHRIST will restore Israel!!! The GREAT
OPPONENT of the God of Israel will fulfil the Lord's
most holy word, and carry out His hallowed covenant. To suit his own wicked purposes he will make
a league with the peculiar people, adhere thereto for
a short time, then *break it in the midst* and be the
instrument of a tribulation, in which Israel shall be
sufferers indeed,—a tribulation such as has not been
since this world was.

For awhile now I shall speak no more of Israel,
but give attention to this ANTICHRIST. Afterwards
the case of Israel will come again before our notice.

In the *twelfth* chapter of REVELATION, on which
we dwelt in our last chapter, we read of "WAR IN
HEAVEN."—"And there was *War in Heaven;*
Michael and his angels fought against the Dragon,
and the Dragon fought and his angels, and prevailed
not; neither was their place found any more in

Heaven. And the great, Dragon *was cast out*, that old serpent, called the Devil and Satan, which deceiveth the whole world, he was cast out *into the Earth* and his angels were cast out with him." This Prophecy concerning "*War in Heaven*" is introduced indeed in the midst of an *allegory*, and may in a certain measure be *itself allegorical.*—Most likely it is so.—But *this* is clear; Satan, *the devil which deceives the world*, is declared to contest some point of serious import, in which the interests of mankind have intimate concern, the Angels of God being his opponents. He is overcome, and cast down upon the earth, and may no longer interfere *except upon its surface.* Whether the contest will be (as it were) army against army,—spiritual beings in array against spiritual beings; or whether it will be, so to speak, the *moral* force of Heaven against 'the *immoral* force of Hell; we cannot know. But *a contest—a war—there will be in some form or other*, and Satan will thenceforth be cast down and confined to earth until the day shall come for his more trying bondage in the pit prepared for his millennial imprisonment. It would appear from many parts of Scripture, that the great Arch-Adversary carries on his work among the sons of men *in our day*, chiefly through the agency of *his unholy Angels,** but in *that day* he will be forced to make this world *his seat;* and here, among mankind, will all his hellish force be concentrated. THUS LIMITED, THE EVIL ONE WILL NOT BE IDLE. He will have *great wrath* because he will know that he hath but a short time.†

* Ephesians vi. 12. † Revelations xii. 12.

What this conquered, but still wrathful one will do we have now to discover.

We venture an *assertion* before proof.—He will in the first place REVEAL THE ANTICHRIST; and then USE HIM AS A MIGHTY INSTRUMENT FOR RAISING UP A FEARFUL POWER OF EVIL. He will *reveal the Antichrist;*—that is, he will TAKE POSSESSION OF AND ENERGIZE A MAN, COMMUNICATING TO HIM ALL HE CAN BESTOW ON OUR MORTALITY, OF FIENDISH POWER AND CRAFT.

"Ye have heard," said St. John, "that Antichrist (THE Antichrist 'Ο' Αντιχριστος) shall come; even now there are many Antichrists;" but this shall be THE ANTICHRIST. This is a *full title;* it means *the* CONTRARY OF CHRIST. The one set over against Christ, as it were *in mimic correspondence,* bearing out the peculiar details of Christ's position and offices in such a manner as to deceive and overthrow the faith of men. So at least the teaching of the Bible leads us to expound the word. For we find there, that—as CHRIST was a *man in-dwelt by* the Eternal God; as ANTICHRIST will be a *man in-dwelt* by Satan; as CHRIST is the *second person in the Trinity in Heaven,* (the Father, the Son, and the Holy Ghost;) so ANTICHRIST will be the *second person in the Trinity of Hell,* (the Devil, the Beast, and the False Prophet,)—as the *Father* gave *not His Spirit by measure unto Christ;* so will not *Satan give his spirit by measure unto Antichrist.* Thus A MAN— the CONTRARY OF CHRIST,—shall practice and prosper in the world.

But so *astounding* and *terrible* an assertion must

not go *unproved*. However there is ample Scripture proof at hand.

I will first ask for your attention to a passage from the *Second Chapter* of the *Second Epistle* to the THESSALONIANS. The Apostle there tells us of a certain "MAN OF SIN" who must be revealed before the end shall come, and whom he calls "THE SON OF PERDITION." He speaks of him as one, "WHO OPPOSETH, AND EXALTETH HIMSELF ABOVE ALL THAT IS CALLED GOD, OR THAT IS WORSHIPPED; SO THAT HE, AS God, SITTETH IN THE TEMPLE OF GOD, SHOWING HIMSELF THAT HE IS GOD." Now we cannot fail to observe, that this proud opposer must be a man *yet to be revealed;* for since St. Paul's day there has been *no Temple of God*, wherein such an one should sit. The Temple at Jerusalem *is not:* and no other Temple has succeeded it, to which we have received a sanction to apply so honored a distinction. ST. PETER'S AT ROME most certainly can lay no claim to such a title with the feeblest ray of justice. Nor can we point to any church or other building in the world which might be singled out amongst its fellows as meriting the name. The Temple of God, therefore, which is spoken of by Paul, must be a temple *yet to be erected.* Now the only temple of which we *read in Scripture* as a temple for God's worship *to be reared again*, is that of which the full particulars are given by EZEKIEL.* But evidently no man of sin will sit in *that* Temple. It is the temple of God pertaining to Jerusalem which will adorn Judea in the happy age of the

* Ezekiel xl. to xlviii.

Millennium, when righteousness and peace will reign
triumphantly beneath the sway of our Emmanuel's
sceptre.   But when Israel are restored to their own
land, we cannot doubt that their *first* act will be
to build their House for worship.   Their occupation
of the Covenant land would be *as nothing*, if their
Temple, their ritual, and their sacrifices, were not
present.   Now, if—upon the old foundations—the
children of the Covenant should rear the Temple and
restore the old Mosaic ritual;—if *there*, the God of
Abraham, (although not acceptably, because without
the faith of Jesus) should be praised; if the Word of
God, (although in part only) should be the word
directing all the services and ceremonies; What
could that Temple be with justice called, except the
"TEMPLE OF GOD"?   Nay, we remember how that
even when the ancient temple reared by Herod on
the old foundation laid by Ezra, was defiled by usury
and hypocrisy, the Lord declared it was "HIS
FATHER'S HOUSE."*   And when the Lord was
crucified and had been preached to, and rejected by,
the Jews; the Apostles, (being Jews themselves) did
not cast off their reverence for the temple worship.
To the Temple went up *Peter* and *John* at the
appointed hour of prayer."†   *There* was *Paul* found
in obedience to the Law :‡ and *thither* he repaired
from time to time "to worship" God.§   To the
Apostles, (though the Temple service did not recog-
nize the Saviour Jesus as the Son of the Most High,)
the Temple was no less THE TEMPLE OF THEIR GOD

---

* John ii—16.   † Acts iii. 1.
‡ Acts xxi. 26.   § Acts xxiv. 11.

AND FATHER. Indeed how *could* it have been otherwise? And how can any future building standing in its place, erected after the pattern shown to Moses in the Mount, erected *by Israel* for the service of the *God of Israel*, be *otherwise?* for did not God say—when the first house was reared by Solomon—"I have hallowed this house . . . to put my name there *for ever;* and mine eyes and my heart—shall be there PERPETUALLY."* There can be then, I think, no doubt whatever that when Paul spoke of *"the man of sin sitting in the Temple of God,"* he meant, that he should sit in a Temple *to be reared and dedicated unto God, the God of Israel, in Jerusalem,* where the Temple built by HEROD was *then* standing, and where that by SOLOMON had stood in days of old: The Temple in which God had put His name "FOR EVER." This proud opposer then must be a man YET TO BE REVEALED.

But farther; He will ASSUME THE POSITION OF GOD. "He, *as God*, sitteth in the Temple of God, *showing himself that* HE IS GOD." And this he will do *by a power not his own*, for we read that his "COMING IS AFTER THE WORKING (xaτ᾽ ἐνεργειαν *i. e.* after the *in*-working) *of Satan, with all power, and signs, and lying wonders, and with all deceivableness of unrighteousness."*

And again; THIS MAN WILL BE ALIVE WHEN CHRIST SHALL COME; for it is he *"whom the Lord shall consume with the spirit of His Mouth, and destroy with the brightness of His coming."*

Thus does the Apostle speak of one to be re-

* 1 Kings ix. 3.

vealed,—"THAT MAN OF SIN,"—who will most certainly deserve the name of "ANTICHRIST."

Now to the same effect is the word of DANIEL. Let us refer to his prophecy, and see how accurately he and the Apostle PAUL agree. In the *Eighth Chapter* we read of a vision in which the Angel Gabriel addressed the Prophet, saying, "Behold I will make thee know what shall be in *the last end of the indignation.*" "When the transgressors are come to the full, a king of fierce countenance and understanding dark sentences shall stand up: And his power shall be mighty, but *not by his own power;* and he shall destroy wonderfully, and shall prosper and practise, and shall destroy the mighty and the holy people. And through his policy also he shall cause craft to prosper in his hand: and he shall *magnify himself in his heart, and by peace shall destroy many; he shall also stand against the Prince of Princes; but he shall be broken without hand.*"*

But let us look for farther corroboration in the *Eleventh chapter* of the same prophet. In this chapter we are carried through a course of events from the time of the Medes and Persians onwards, until the reign of a certain King, who, arising from a low estate—a vile person†—shall make a "league" with Israel;‡ "work deceitfully;" "enter peaceably even upon the fattest places of the province;" and do "that which his fathers have not done, nor his fathers' fathers; .... *he shall pollute the sanctuary of strength, and shall take away the daily sacrifice, and shall place*

---

* Daniel viii. 19—25. † Daniel xi. 21.
‡ Compare Daniel xi. 23, with Daniel ix. 27.

the abomination that maketh desolate:" he shall cause the people who "do know their God," and "understand," to "fall by the sword and by flame, by captivity and by spoil: . . . . he shall do according to his will, and he shall *exalt himself, and magnify himself above every God*, and shall *speak marvellous things against the God of gods*, and shall prosper till the indignation be accomplished." "He shall plant the tabernacle of his palace between the seas in the glorious holy mountain; yet he shall come to his end and none shall help him. *And at that time shall Michael stand up*. . . . . And there shall be a time of trouble such as never was since there was a nation," and at that time shall the people written in God's book "be delivered," and the first resurrection (as explained before)* shall take place.†

Thus PAUL and DANIEL agree accurately. They both present for our contemplation a "MAN OF SIN" to be revealed in "*the last time:*"—A MAN CLAIMING FOR HIMSELF THE HONOR DUE TO THE ALMIGHTY, AND EXERCISING MORE THAN HUMAN POWER *because indwelt by Satan—A King, moreover, standing up against the Prince of Princes*, to be destroyed when He appears in glory—AN ANTICHRIST, therefore, indeed.

Now no man can assert that such an one as here is mentioned has *yet* reigned upon the earth. It is idle to speak of the *Roman Empire*, or *Antiochus Epiphanes*, or the *Papacy*. No one surely, who will examine honestly what Paul and Daniel have predicted can be otherwise than well convinced that the

* See Chapter II.　　† Daniel xi., xii.

King spoken of is a man of deep, dark mystery, who is YET TO BE REVEALED.

Having found so much information on the sacred page concerning the GREAT EVIL ONE who is to reign as King upon the earth, let us dwell awhile on the POSITION and PECULIARITY of his kingdom and government, that we may see clearly, not only that he is *An* Antichrist, but THE GREAT ANTICHRIST especially foretold.

We will leave the Prophet Daniel for awhile, and take the testimony of ISAIAH. In the *fourteenth chapter* of his prophecy, we have BABYLON; *Babylon of the last days*—brought before us; The Babylon, *upon the overthrow of which* the prophet says—"*the whole earth is at rest and is quiet, they break forth into singing.*" No doubt therefore it is the same Babylon as that dwelt upon in the seventeenth and eighteenth chapters of REVELATION, "that great city Babylon, that mighty city" with which the Kings of the earth "have committed fornication and lived deliciously;" wherein is merchandise of gold, and silver, and precious stones, and pearls, and fine linen, and purple . . . . and odours, and ointments, and frankincense, and wine, and oil . . . . and chariots, and slaves, and souls of men;" that "MYSTERY, BABYLON THE GREAT, THE MOTHER OF HARLOTS AND ABOMINATIONS OF THE EARTH."

Now the Prophet ISAIAH in this fourteenth chapter speaks much concerning the LAST KING thereof. He views that monarch at the *end* of his career, and says—"Hell from beneath is moved for thee to meet

thee at thy coming: it stirreth up the dead for thee."
He portrays all the kings of the nations lying in their
graves astonished at his overthrow. "Art *thou* become weak as *we?* Art *thou* become as one of *us?*
How art thou fallen from Heaven, O Lucifer, son of
the morning! How art *thou* cut down to the ground
which didst weaken the nations. For thou hast said
in thine heart, I will ascend into Heaven, I will exalt
my throne above the stars of God; I will ascend
above the heights of the clouds; I will be *like the
Most High.* Yet thou shalt be brought down to Hell,
to the sides of the pit. . . . . The Lord of Hosts hath
sworn, saying, Surely, as I have thought, so it shall
come to pass; and as I have purposed, so shall it
stand; that I will break the Assyrian IN MY LAND,
and UPON MY MOUNTAINS will I tread him under foot.
Then shall his yoke depart from off them, and his
burden depart from off their shoulders. This is the
purpose that is proposed *upon the whole earth;* and
this is the hand which is stretched out *upon all nations.*"

Such was the burden which Isaiah was commissioned to proclaim concerning this last monarch "in
the year that King Ahaz died;" and thus, though not
with the same fulness of detail, does he foretell his
reign of terror in entire agreement both with Daniel
and St. Paul, specifying in prophetic symbol, the
great nation he shall rule: The BABYLONISH EMPIRE
of the *prophetic word: the* ROME *of History.*

But is it so? Are we right in thus deciding that
his empire will be ROMAN? Let us carefully examine. Again we will refer to DANIEL, the *seventh*

chapter. Here we find laid down in order FOUR SEPARATE KINGDOMS bearing prominent rule in the world in different periods of its, then future, history. These kingdoms are exhibited under the emblem of four beasts with distinguishing characteristics, and upon the expiration of the time allotted to the fourth beast, a FIFTH kingdom is brought forward, namely, "THE KINGDOM OF THE PEOPLE OF THE SAINTS OF THE MOST HIGH." Now we need hardly pause to explain to any who have sought to understand their Bible, that there have been four great Empires, holding their dominion as the Empires of the world, beginning with the time of Daniel: namely the BABYLONIAN, the MEDO-PERSIAN, the GRECIAN, and the ROMAN. Dwelling upon the FOURTH of these kingdoms, Daniel's prophecy informs us, that it shall be *diverse* from all kingdoms, and shall devour the whole earth, and tread it down, and break it in pieces."

That such was the case with the ROMAN EMPIRE, we know. But farther;—"The ten horns out of this kingdom are *ten kings* that shall arise." Now it is remarkable that from very early times down to our own day, the number of Kingdoms associated with Rome has been *ten.* If we go back as far as the fourth or fifth century, or if we descend to the eighth, the twelfth, the sixteenth, or the nineteenth, we shall find them to have been *ten,* until the recent Italian war, when the bond appears to have been broken,*

* It appears that just before the war between France and Austria, when Napoleon III. took so active a part in the affairs of Italy, the Kingdoms or States *speaking in the Latin tongue* and *bearing allegiance to the Roman Creed,* were ten in number: France, Spain, Portugal, Austria, Sardinia, Tuscany, Modena, Parma, The States of the Church, and Naples.

for reasons which we shall understand presently. But to pursue the language of the prophecy,—"And *another* (that is another king) shall arise after them: and he shall be diverse from the first, and shall *subdue three kings.*" Now surely this seals the matter at once *against* THE PAPACY *being offered* to our notice, as represented by this last king. The Papal power cannot be spoken of with peculiar note, as having *subdued three kingdoms.* For this, we need but see how *greatly* commentators *differ* in their attempts to establish, such a subjugation as a point of history. Moreover, this eleventh king was to arise *after* the ten. But the ten have endured till *now.* Therefore he who shall come *after* them *cannot be the Papacy,* and forasmuch as such a king does not yet appear, his reign *must* be still FUTURE. But further, —"And he shall speak great swelling words against the Most High, and shall wear out the Saints of the Most High, and think to change times and laws; and they shall be given into his hand, until a time, and times, and the dividing of time. But the judgment shall sit, and they shall take away his dominion, to consume and to destroy it unto the end. And the kingdom and dominion, and the greatness of the kingdom under the whole Heaven, shall be given to the people of the Saints of the Most High."

Here then we have the period of this king's reign marked *definitely.* It shall be at the *close* of the time which is allotted to the *fourth great kingdom,* namely the ROMAN.

But is this clear also on reference to other parts of Scripture? We will refer to the *following chapter*

6

√

(*the eighth*).   In the *nineteenth verse* the period to
which the grand point of the prophecy had reference,
is distinctly named "THE LAST END OF THE INDIGNA-
TION."   We *then* have laid before us a sketch directing our attention to the kingdom of the Medes and
Persians, and that of Alexander the Great, whose
dominions were divided into four parts after his death.
("*Four kingdoms shall stand up out of the nation, but
not in his power.*"*)   And then passing on to "the
latter time of their kingdom when the transgressors
are come to the full," it is said that "a king of fierce
countenance and understanding dark sentences shall
stand up," of whose character we have been already
speaking.   Now "THE LATTER TIME OF THEIR KING-
DOM" must be the time of the fourth great kingdom
of the world,—THE ROMAN: for the Romans gradually
obtained dominion over all the countries which the
four joint successors of Alexander governed.   Egypt
(the last subjugated of the four) being made a province of the Roman Empire B. C. 30.

Thus, that the King of fierce countenance shall
have dominion over the Roman Empire, is shown in

---

* It may be well to call to memory what these four kingdoms
were. The *first* was composed of Armenia, Media, Babylonia,
Syria, Susiana, a portion of Cappadocia, and Cilicia. This kingdom,
indeed, claimed an extension from India to the Hellespont. The
second comprehended a part of Thrace, Asia Minor, part of Cappadocia, and the countries which were within the limits of Mount
Taurus. The *third* consisted of Macedonia, Thessaly, and part of
Greece. The *fourth* spread over part of Asia Minor, part of Thrace,
Cœlo-Syria, Phœnicia, Palestine, Cyprus, Cyrene and Egypt. The
first Kings were Alexander's four Generals—Seleucus Nicator,
Lysimachus, Cassander, and Ptolemy, who ruled over these four
kingdoms respectively.

this place also. But so far being clear from the testimony of the Prophets, let us seek for a more detailed account in the *New Testament*.

We will refer to REVELATION, the *thirteenth* chapter. This chapter is occupied with the affairs of "that great City Babylon, which reigneth over the kings of the earth." The Lord here brings before us two allegorical figures—"Beasts," or living creatures. The first arises "out OF THE SEA." It has "SEVEN HEADS and TEN HORNS, and on its heads THE NAMES OF BLASPHEMY." Now there is certainly a great probability that ROME is represented by this figure—ROME IMPERIAL. ROME, *the* SEAT *of the Empire*, the point indeed from which the Empire sprang, is situated *between the Seas*. It has had *Seven forms of Government* having their *seat* always at the ancient Capital. These forms of Government were as follows:—KINGS—CONSULS—DICTATORS—DECEMVIRS—CONSULAR TRIBUNES,—EMPERORS,—and POPES. And (as we have already seen) it has been peculiarly characterized by the association, at least for many centuries—of TEN KINGDOMS under its control, or closely bound to its interests. But we read that when "*power* and a *seat* and *great authority*" had been given by Satan to this Beast,—"*one of its heads was, as it were, wounded unto death; and his deadly wound was healed*, and all the world wondered after the beast." This was true of Rome. The SIXTH head,—that of the EMPERORS,—was wounded unto death, by the sword of foreign invaders. It grew *weaker and weaker*, until the *name* of Emperor and no more, existed. Yet, notwithstanding this, the nation did not actually *expire*. The capital was held by one who wore the diadem, as *King of all the Kings of Earth;* and wonderful authority he exercised. The wounded beast *did live*, for the PAPACY kept it alive. It was indeed quite changed in character, and not acknowledged in the world as the old Roman Empire. Still it lived and flourished, for *"The deadly wound was healed;"* and all the world wondered after the beast. "And they worshipped the dragon which gave power unto the beast, and they worshipped the beast, saying, Who is like unto the beast? Who is able to make war with him?" And now again, we are told, "there was given unto him a mouth speaking great things and blasphemies; and power was given unto him to continue *forty and two months* . . . . to make war with the saints, and to overcome them, and power was given him over all kindreds, and tongues, and nations." Now if we accept (and there surely is no just reason why we should not accept) the usual interpretation; the "forty and two months" are to be considered to be months of *years;* that is, *each day* therein is to be reckoned *as a year.* Thus we have *one thousand two hundred and sixty years* for the duration of the Papacy as a headship of the Roman Empire.* Now it is worthy of *remark* certainly, and of *serious thought* also, that from the Edict of Justinian (A.D. 533) which gave political power to the Pope of Rome, (and from the date of which edict the Papal Empire grew with rapid strides) to the well-known year 1793, when the Papacy lost its imperial authority (and from which time it has grown

* See Chapter X.

only more and more contemptible in a political aspect), was *twelve hundred and sixty years,* or *forty and two* months. The Papacy is still a power—alas! but NOT IMPERIAL. It has no authority which it can exercise over any King in Europe. For this its day is *gone.* But let us see now what is further stated in the word before us. "And I beheld ANOTHER BEAST coming up OUT OF THE EARTH; and he had *two horns* like a *lamb,* and he spake as a *dragon.*" Let us remark that this second beast does not arise from the *sea;* his seat is not *Italy;* but INLAND; he comes up "OUT OF THE EARTH;" he has *two horns* like a lamb." Not like Rome having an association of *ten* Kings, but TWO ONLY. A dynasty, possibly, of TWO MONARCHS. The likeness to *a lamb,* may indicate a remarkable appearance of *peacefulness;* while his speech being like that of *a dragon* represents *cruelty.*" It may be, "he shall come in peaceably and obtain the kingdom by flatteries," and "work deceitfully;"* so that "by peace he shall destroy many."† This beast, is to "exercise all the power of the first beast before him;" that is, he is to be head of the Roman Empire, though his dwelling is not found between the seas. Moreover he is to *do honor to the first beast.* He shall cause "the earth and them which dwell therein to *worship him;* that is, we may suppose *to bow down submissively to the Imperial authority* as of old. But more:—This new beast "*doeth wonders,*" so that he maketh fire come down from Heaven on the earth in the sight of men, and *deceiveth them that dwell on the earth by means of those miracles which he had power to do*

* Daniel xi. 21—23.   † Daniel viii. 25.

IN THE SIGHT OF.THE BEAST," (that is in the sight of the *whole Empire.*)   And besides this, "he causeth all both small and great, rich and poor, free and bond, to receive a mark in their right hand or in their foreheads, and that no man might buy or sell, save he that had the mark or the name of the beast, or the number of his name."   And it is added—"Here is wisdom;—Let him that hath understanding count the number of the beast; for it is the number of A MAN: and his number is SIX HUNDRED THREE SCORE AND SIX.*

* Revelation xiii.

* It may be interesting to the readers of these chapters to note the following words, in Hebrew, Greek, and Latin, each of which, by the use of their letters as figures, will spell 666.

1 רומיית (Romiith) the fem. of רומי agreeing with מלכות (a kingdom) the Roman Kingdom.

2 Ἡ Λατίνη Βασιλεία the Latin Kingdom.

8 Λατεινος a Latin person.

4 Ναπολεοντι the dative *dedicatory* form of writing Napoleon.

5 *LVDOVICVS* (Louis).

The following table will show this to be correct:

1		2		3		4		5	
ר	.. 200	η	.. 8	λ	.. 30	ν	.. 50	L	.. 50
ו	.. 6	λ	.. 30	α	.. 1	α	.. 1	V	.. 5
מ	.. 40	α	.. 1	τ	.. 300	π	.. 80	D	.. 500
י	.. 10	τ	.. 300	ε	.. 5	ο	.. 70	O	.. 0
י	.. 10	ι	.. 10	ι	.. 10	λ	.. 80	V	.. 5
ת	.. 400	ν	.. 50	ν	.. 50	ε	.. 5	I	.. 1
		η	.. 8	ο	.. 70	ο	.. 70	C	.. 100
		β	.. 2	ς	.. 200	ν	.. 50	V	.. 5
		α	.. 1			τ	.. 300	S	.. 0
		σ	.. 200			ι	.. 10		
		ι	.. 10						
		λ	.. 30						
		ε	.. 5						
		ι	.. 10						
		α	.. 1						
	666		666		666		666		666

Now upon this second beast I will but comment briefly. We know the dynasty which rose to power in *inland parts,* and at the close of the last century laid hands on the Imperial throne, taking all *but the name only* from the Papacy, depriving him, who held the Imperial title by the Pope's authority, even of the empty name in which he gloried.* That dynasty still holds the sceptre, still has control at Rome, and how it will develope itself there and elsewhere, GOD ALONE CAN TELL.

But we have another very clear and powerful word upon this subject in the *seventeenth chapter.*

A woman is spoken of "*sitting on* MANY WATERS," (elsewhere described as meaning "peoples and multitudes, and nations and tongues.")† The woman is arrayed in purple and scarlet, decked with gold and precious stones, and pearls, having a golden cup in her hand, full of abominations, and upon her forehead a name written—"MYSTERY, BABYLON THE GREAT, THE MOTHER OF HARLOTS, AND ABOMINATIONS OF THE EARTH."

* The Emperor Napoleon I. degraded the Pope to the rank of Bishop of Rome; stripped the See of Rome of all its temporalities; and confiscated its Revenues of every kind. The note was struck in 1793. In 1798, the blood of the Roman clergy was shed like water, the city Rome was taken, and the Pope (Pius VI.) was led away captive. In 1809, the temporal sovereignty of Rome and the States of the Church was taken by General Radet, in the name of Napoleon, who divided the States into departments, to be governed by French officers; and the Emperor conferred on his infant son the title of King of Rome. Thus the Papacy, as an Imperial power, received a blow from which it has not rallied.—*See Hale's Chronology, Vol. 3, pp. 625, 626, and Keith's World and Church, pp.* 214—217.

† Verse 15.

She appears, drunken with the blood of the Saints and the Martyrs of Jesus." Now every one reading this description of the woman, is ready to decide at once "THIS IS THE PAPACY." And no doubt *it is so.* But it is NOT "*The Antichrist.*" It is NOT "*The Man of Sin.*" It may be a *type* of him, but it is *not he.* But let us observe what is said about the woman. In the third verse we read thus,—"He carried me away into *the wilderness; and I saw the* woman *sit upon a scarlet colored beast.*" Her place and position are *changed.* She *had been* "sitting upon MANY WATERS," (*i. e., ruling over many nations.*) But *now* she has *left her* position of authority, and we find her *in the wilderness, supported by a scarlet-colored beast,* full of names of blasphemy, having SEVEN HEADS AND TEN HORNS: she is supported, therefore, by the same beast which came before us as the *first* beast in the *thirteenth chapter,* namely, THE ROMAN EMPIRE. Then we have here the Roman Empire *supporting* the Papacy; the Papacy, as it would appear, *having become too weak to support itself.* But an explanation is afforded us in this chapter, which makes it very plain that only the *last headship* of this Empire is the supporter. In the *seventh verse* we find the Angel saying to St. John,—"I will tell thee the mystery of the woman, and of the beast that carrieth her, which hath the seven heads and ten horns. The beast that thou sawest WAS, and IS NOT: and shall ascend out of the bottomless pit, and go into perdition: and they that dwell on the earth shall wonder, whose names were not written in the book of life from the foundation of the world, when they behold THE BEAST THAT *WAS* AND *IS NOT*, AND *YET IS*. And here is the mind that hath wisdom. The *seven heads* are seven mountains on which the woman sitteth." (*Rome is built on seven hills*) "and there are seven Kings," (*this we have explained already in this chapter.*) "Five are fallen." (*In St. John's day—five of the forms of Government had passed away; viz., Kings, Consuls, Dictators, Decemvirs, and Consular-Tribunes.*) "One is"—(*the form of government in the days of the Apostle John was that of an Empire; Emperors ruled.*) "And the other is not yet come, and when he cometh he must *continue* a short space." (*When the Empire was wounded unto death, the Papacy took the reins of government, stepping in gradually to take its place, and heal the wound, and soon, assuming full imperial functions, gave away kingdoms, and treated Kings as vassals. It continued forty and two months, that is (taking a day for a year)* TWELVE HUNDRED AND SIXTY YEARS, *when it likewise was compelled to resign the Throne and give way to another power.* "And the BEAST THAT WAS, AND IS NOT, even he is the *eighth* and is *of the seven;* (*he does not* SEEM *to be of the seven; he is not* CALLED *either Emperor, or Pope, or King, but he is in truth* THE HEAD *nevertheless. But what have we here? A dynasty* RISING INTO POWER; *then* PASSING AWAY; *and then* RISING AGAIN. As to this dynasty, we have but one word further. It is joined, like the Empire of old, by TEN KINGS, and they *make war with the Lamb;* and unite together also to *consume the Papacy* which they had supported. They conspire, in fact, to cast out of the world ALL RELIGION, except that idol worship, THAT WORSHIP OF THE BEAST HIMSELF, which he will set up "in the temple of God," where he will show himself that "*he is God.*" And finally, having fulfilled his day, like those who preceded him, he shall "GO INTO PERDITION" together with the "FALSE PROPHET" who will work miracles before him; to be followed in God's own good time by the remaining person of the Antichristian trinity,—THE DRAGON (that is SATAN,) who must be reserved a little while, though bound and by a lengthy bondage kept from carrying on his work of evil. Apart then from the help we might derive from the prophetic *dates*, we can perceive, without *much* room for doubt, *if any*, from WHAT QUARTER we must look for the LAST KING; the Great Opponent of the Lord; the "Idol Shepherd;" the Great Deceiver; "the Antichrist." It is evident that he pertains to the EIGHTH DYNASTY OF THE ROMAN HEADSHIP; THE VERY DYNASTY UNDER WHICH—AS IT APPEARS—WE LIVE. Therefore we may safely think we are not *very* far from THAT GREAT DAY, WHEN EVERY BELIEVER SHALL BEHOLD HIS LORD.

But now there is another point which we must notice, before we quit this subject of the *reign of Antichrist.* I mean, HIS DEALINGS WITH THE JEWISH PEOPLE, of whose restoration we were led to speak particularly in the earlier part of this chapter.

Let us refer once more to DANIEL'S prophecy.

Much difference has arisen among prophetical

interpreters, concerning the SEVENTY WEEKS spoken of in the *ninth chapter*. It is said "SEVENTY WEEKS are determined upon thy people, and upon thy holy city, to finish the transgression, and to make an end of sins, and to make reconciliation for iniquity, and to bring in everlasting righteousness, and to seal up the vision and prophecy, and to anoint the Most Holy." Let us dwell for a moment on this passage, before we proceed. "*Seventy weeks*" (taken, as the necessity of the case obliges, a day for a year;— equal therefore to *four hundred and ninety years*) "are determined (נֶחְתַּךְ cut off, divided) upon *thy people*" (Daniel's people, the Jews) "And upon *thy holy city*" (Jerusalem) "To finish" (כלא shut up, restrain) "The transgression" (i. e. of thy people and city) "And to make an end of (חתם to seal up "sins, and to make reconciliation for (כפר to cover) iniquity and to bring in everlasting righteousness, and to seal up the vision and the prophecy, and to anoint the Most Holy" (קדֹשׁ—קדֹשׁים. Whether this expression refers to "*the Holy of Holies*" in the Temple, or to "*the Messiah Himself*, does not appear certain; but it is only right to state that if it have reference to the *Messiah*, it is *the only case* in which this expression, which is used in nearly *thirty places* in the Old Testament, is applied to a person.

Now we know well that scarcely any of these points can yet be looked upon as fulfilled. *The transgression of the Jews*, is not by any means *restrained*, *shut up*, or *finished*: for they reject the Lord as firmly as they ever did, and as truly do they glory in denying Him. *Their sins* are not *sealed up*,

nor *made an end of*, but they are as patent to all the
world as are the sins of the Gentiles. *Reconciliation*
truly is *offered*, because the atonement is complete
through the sacrifice of Christ, but it is not *made*.
There is not reconciliation yet between the Lord and
Israel: their *iniquity* is not *covered*, though the
covering is all in readiness. *Everlasting righteousness* is not *brought in* amongst the tribes of Israel,
for hitherto they have made choice of sin. *The
vision and prophecy* are not yet fulfilled, nor sealed,—
but open, as of old, to the expectation of God's
waiting people. *The Holy of Holies* is not yet
anointed, for their temple is *not yet erected;* nor
is the *Most Holy One*,—the great Messiah,—yet
anointed King, for (as our daily prayer bears constant witness) Messiah's kingdom has *not come*."
So I CANNOT THINK with some interpreters, that the
SEVENTY WEEKS HAVE YET EXPIRED. But let us
follow onward with the subject. "Know therefore
and understand," said the angel, "that from the
going forth of the commandment to restore and
re-build Jerusalem unto Messiah the Prince, shall be
seven weeks and three-score and two weeks, (that is
four hundred and eighty-three years, taking, as
before, a day to represent a year) . . . And after
three-score and two weeks SHALL MESSIAH BE CUT
OFF, BUT NOT FOR HIMSELF. This brings us to
a definite period:—The cutting off of Messiah:—*the
crucifixion of our Lord*. What then was to follow?
The word continues, "And the people of the prince
that shall come, shall destroy the city and the sanctuary." Now we know that the people who destroyed

Jerusalem and its Temple, were ROMANS. THE PRINCE REFERRED TO, WAS THEREFORE TO BE A RO-MAN ALSO. But further it is said—"And the end thereof shall be with a flood, and unto the end of the war desolations are determined." And it *was so* ASSUREDLY. But here the matter has been resting ever since. The war ended in the dispersion of the sons of Judah till the times of the Gentiles should be fulfilled. But with the Gentiles, nay with *Christians* (as such) this prophecy has *nothing whatever to do.* The seventy weeks were determined upon *Daniel's people,*—the Jews,—*and no other.* In looking there-fore for the *remaining week,*—THE LAST WEEK OF THE SEVENTY,—we must keep our eyes upon the day, *yet future,* when "the times of the Gentiles" shall have been accomplished. Then shall "THE PRINCE" of that people which beforetime destroyed the city and the Temple, come forward on behalf of Israel. "And he shall confirm the (a) covenant with many for *one week,* that is—of course—for *seven* years. And *in the midst of the week* he shall cause the sacrifice and the oblation to cease, and for the over-spreading of abominations he shall make it desolate *even until the consummation.* The Prince, then, who will make the covenant must be A DECEIVER. *One who will not keep his word.* He will make a cove-nant with all appearance of strength and security for seven years, and *break it in the midst of the time, that he may overspread the land with abominations, and until the end appointed, make it desolate.* Who now shall this Roman Prince or leader be, who shall act thus toward Israel? Who indeed but that DREAD

BEING, that "MAN OF SIN" of whom we have been speaking.

Surely then we have a hint as to the meaning of our Saviour's word,—"IF ANOTHER SHALL COME IN HIS OWN NAME, HIM YE WILL RECEIVE."* This last head of the Roman Empire will probably be THE FALSE MESSIAH OF THE JEWS, and thus, in very perfect sense, "THE ANTICHRIST." But now, the Covenant made,—the Jews brought to their land under his protection,—the Temple and the sacrificial rites restored: and now *again*, the *covenant broken*, and the sacrifice and oblation caused to cease, in the midst of the seven years: THREE YEARS AND A HALF, ("a time, times, and the dividing of time," will remain, as Daniel predicted)† being left for the full display of all the horrors of the Antichrist's dominion: his gross unparalleled idolatry, his bitter cruelty, his craft, his thirst for blood. But he shall come to his end; for MICHAEL the great Prince shall stand up for *Israel's remnant.* Yea, the Lord shall come and all His Saints attending him, and this "Man of Sin" shall be consumed. But the destruction of Antichrist and the reception of Israel's remnant by the Lord Jesus, must be reserved for the next chapter. To enter upon them would oblige us to bring forward matter which has properly to do with the subjects next in order, viz., THE ADVENT, and THE JUDGMENT OF THE NATIONS.

Let it suffice for the present, that Israel will be indeed restored, *at least in part,* and that in UNBELIEF, *under the auspices of* ANTICHRIST; that they will

* John v. 43.   † Daniel vii. 25.

erect their Temple and restore their Ancient worship; but that their protector will turn speedily against them, and they will endure a tribulation, of a kind more bitter than all former trials.

Now, in concluding this chapter, let me impress upon my readers THE GREAT NEED OF PRAYER ON THE BEHALF OF ISRAEL. We have seen already, and in our future chapters shall see more particularly, what great blessings God has laid in store for the Twelve Tribes in the Millennial age. But they have *much to suffer first*. We must, then, keep them in remembrance.

Moreover, while we pray for them, let us look well also AT HOME: examining OUR OWN standing before God. For even now are there many Antichrists, fore-runners of "THE ANTICHRIST" who shall appear. INFIDELITY is an Antichrist: POPERY and TRACTARIANISM are Antichrists: ANTINOMIANISM is an Antichrist: LUKEWARMNESS is an Antichrist. Let us see that we take not the side of any such, but ever guard our hearts with prayer and watchfulness: ever keep our lives in harmony with the inspired word: ever KEEP OUR BEST AFFECTIONS FIXED WITH FIRMNESS ON THE SAVIOUR. O that in every one of us professed believers there were more DECISION FOR THE LORD: and less room allowed for any man to doubt about us, whose we are and whom we serve. O that we were *more entirely* and *more simply* looking to THE CRUCIFIED ONE, *whose blood alone can cleanse our sins away.* For, *so*, should we stand firmer; *so*, become more joyous; *so*, delight ourselves more fully in the prospect of that day when Christ shall call His people hence; and *so*, if we should see the tribes of Israel returning to their land, we should look up, and lift our heads expectantly, well knowing by that fore-appointed sign, that the Archangel's blast must quickly sound to summon all the servants of the Lord whose glorious "REDEMPTION DRAWETH NIGH."

CHAPTER IV.

THE ADVENT.

"Behold, He cometh with clouds, and every eye shall see Him, and they also which pierce1 Him; and all kindreds of the Earth shall wail because of Him. Even so, Amen."—REV. i. 7.

IT will be needful for us to retrace our steps a little, in order that we may deal fairly with the subject which now comes before us. That subject is THE ADVENT.

Uplifting first the mind *towards Heaven*, we must behold our Great Redeemer, there enthroned in glory at the right hand of the Eternal Father. He is a man, bone of our bone and flesh of our flesh; a man, who once was dead, but liveth, and has been exalted above all the Principalities and Powers of Heaven; a man, before whose GLORIFIED HUMANITY the angels bow. *A man*, yet GOD :* the very and Eternal God: "for whom are all things and by whom all things consist."† Since, in the sight of His disciples He ascended up on high, His session has been there. And there, amid unceasing praises, He must sit—the great High Priest—the only "Mediator between God and men"—until the day appointed by the Father, when He shall descend once more to Earth for JUDG-MENT and SALVATION.

---

* John i. 1—3. Romans ix. 5. † Col. i. 16, 17.

7

In Heaven, then, at the right hand of power, awaiting the appointed time, let us BEHOLD OUR LORD as we commence this chapter. And let us note well the fact,—*He shall descend to Earth again.* HE SHALL DESCEND. That once despised and rejected Lord who by the hand of wickedness was crucified, but who, by the Eternal Spirit rose again, and then ascended, and now sits enthroned at the right hand of power—THAT VERY JESUS, at the time appointed, SHALL DESCEND as King and Judge UPON OUR FALLEN EARTH.

Moreover, it is evident that He will come AS MAN; clothed indeed in the *perfection* of our manhood, but still in its *reality.* It does not require much searching into Scripture to establish this. In the *first chapter* of THE ACTS OF THE APOSTLES we are told that when Jesus had spoken His last words to His disciples, "while they beheld, He was taken up, and a cloud received Him out of their sight. And while they looked steadfastly towards Heaven, as He went up, behold two men stood by them in white apparel, which said, ye men of Galilee why stand ye gazing up into Heaven? THIS SAME JESUS which is taken up from you into Heaven, shall *so come in like manner as ye have seen Him go into Heaven.*" "THIS SAME JESUS," then, who had arisen from the grave, who had been crucified, who had dwelt and ministered among the sons of men; who had been born of a human mother in Bethlehem;—THIS SAME JESUS, shall most surely come again "*in like manner*" as He went. *Descending* instead of *ascending;* the clouds unfolding to *reveal* His manhood, instead of closing round about, *to hide it* from our sight.

But now let us follow the ALMIGHTY SAVIOUR by the steps of His descent.

"The MAN CHRIST JESUS" quits the Throne of Intercession at the right hand of Heaven, and advances towards the Earth. The glory of the Father's Majesty surrounds Him. The Holy Angels bear Him company.* Thus, to an appointed place in heights above the world, He makes descent, and there *a pause ensues.*† The trumpet sounds in the hearing of the DEAD *in Christ*, that they arise from vaulted tomb, and earth, and stream, and sea, to meet Him. It sounds, moreover, in the hearing of the LIVING SAINTS that their frail mortal put on immortality, and that they ascend to be for ever with the Lord. And they obey the summons. On this "first resurrection" we have dwelt before; we need not speak of it, therefore, in further explanation. THUS, however, does the LAST GREAT DAY—the DAY OF THE LORD'S ADVENT —open.

But when the multitudes who have arisen and ascended to their Lord, are in His presence, *what shall follow?* Surely eye of man hath never seen, nor ear heard, nor heart conceived—the JOY, the BLISS, the GLORY!!! O think of the re-union of those loving ones the grave has so long severed! Husbands and wives, parents and children, friends and friends, united now to live and love FOR EVER! No more to shed a tear! no more to doubt, nor sin, nor suffer! No friend to cause another pang of grief to friend! The name of enemy unknown! All perfect peace, rest; joy, praise, glory, *everlastingly*. And then the

---

* Matt. xxv. 31. Mark viii. 38.   † Thess. iv. 16, 17. Rev. xix.

brightness!—O, the brightness of the Hosts of Heaven!—those HOLY ANGELS, close attendants on the King of Kings, each one so beautiful, so good, so full of love. To have such beings for companions! To converse with them of all the marvels of redeeming grace! To hear their words declare the praises of *their* Lord and *ours!* How wonderful! But then again—more glorious still—The vision of THE GREAT ALMIGHTY KING! "The King in His beauty!" "The altogether lovely!!" To gaze upon his glory *now*, would be beyond endurance. We cannot look upon the face of God and live.* But *then* we shall have power to look upon Him, and beholding Him arrayed in all the brightness of the Father's glory, shall have grace *to praise Him* as the holy angels do, and *love Him* with a love which those alone can exercise whose once sin-ruined souls have been redeemed and saved.

But let us glance just for a moment at OURSELVES as we shall be when thus we look upon, and love, and praise Him. OURSELVES—*in new array—how changed! how wholly changed!* this frail corruption having put on incorruption, and this weak mortal, immortality,† no longer shall we bear the stamp of sin, or its sad consequences, but we shall be *like the Lord.* It is not said we shall be like the *angels*, but we shall be like *the Lord*—LIKE CHRIST!!!"‡ washed in His blood, clothed in His righteousness, made holy by His Spirit, complete in Him. Not only so, but more—we shall be GLORIFIED TOGETHER WITH HIM IN HIS OWN TRANSCENDENT GLORY. "SONS, more-

---

* Exodus xxxiii. 20.   † 1 Cor. xv. 53.   ‡ 1 John iii. 2.

over, in His Sonship; KINGS, in His Kingship;—
PRIESTS, in His Priesthood."* O what a blissful
sequel to the toils and griefs of earth!!! *Can we
now see our title clearly to this blessed state?* Would
this glory be *our* portion if the Lord were to come
NOW? If not,—*O why not?* Not because of any
want of love or grace on GOD'S part. Far from it;
for there is a FULL and FREE SALVATION through the
faith of Jesus, offered to each sinner upon Earth..
Christ died *for all*, and God wills *all men* to be
saved.† O search the Scriptures; see if such a thing
can be as a Believer in Christ Jesus lost. Nay, you
will but search *in vain*. IT CANNOT BE; thank God.
"As Moses lifted up the serpent in the wilderness,
even so is the Redeemer lifted up, that WHOSOEVER
BELIEVETH IN HIM should not perish but have everlasting life."‡ Let US *believe* then,—fellow travellers
to eternity,—*believe in the Lord Jesus Christ*, AND
WE SHALL LIVE, yea LIFE IS OURS, a life which cannot
end, it is the PRESENT—the IMMEDIATE—portion of
the weakest child of faith."§

But now in this estate of glory we must leave the
Saints of Jesus for the present, that we may observe
some of the great events which will transpire upon
the Earth.

If not *before* the resurrection and translation of
"the First Fruits,"‖ at any rate *soon after* they are
gathered to their Lord, the Reign of the last king, AS
ANTICHRIST, will commence, and the persecution of

---

* John xvii. 22. Rom. viii. 14—17. Rev. i. 6. Rev. iii. 21.
† 2 Cor. v. 14, 15. 2 Tim. ii. 4. Heb. ii. 9.   ‡ John iii. xiv. 15.
§ John iii. 36, vi. 47, xi. 25, 26.   ‖ See Chapter II.

the Saints upon the Earth be set on foot. The Jews will then discover their grand error: the Covenant will be broken: and "the day of Jacob's trouble" be revealed. GOD, by the hand of Antichrist, will have gathered them into Jerusalem and be about to blow upon them in the fire of His wrath, and melt them in the midst thereof. But the distress will be *effectual:* for the Spirit of Grace and Supplication will be poured on them from Heaven, and they will look on Him whom they have pierced and mourn for Him, as one mourneth for his only son, and shall be in bitterness for him, as one that is in bitterness for his first-born. "In that day there shall be a great mourning in Jerusalem .... and the land shall mourn, every family apart .... *all the families that remain*, every family apart, and their wives apart." And "in that day there shall be a fountain opened to the house of David and the to inhabitants of Jerusalem, for sin and for uncleanness." And God will bring *a third part* through the fire, and will refine them as silver is refined, and will try them as gold is tried; they shall call on His name and He will hear them; He will say, "*it is my people;*" and they shall say, "*the Lord is my God.*"* Thus will the remnant of Israel be brought to repentance at the last hour, and be permitted, *at the very Advent itself*, to look on Him whom they pierced and obtain life through His name. There will "in that day" be a fountain open for sin "to the house of David and to the inhabitants of Jerusalem," *and the destroying angels will allow the third of those among God's covenanted people who had been deceived by*

* Zech. xii. 10—14, xiii. 1, 2.

Antichrist, to live. They will be left amongst the remnant whom the Lord will spare, to people the millennial Earth.

But now another great event is brought before us, in connection with the Saviour's Advent:—namely, THE DESTRUCTION OF "BABYLON" THE "MYSTERY." The exact position of Great Babylon's overthrow with respect to the time of Israel's trouble and the Advent of the Lord is, I think, clear. It will be *immediately* upon the manifestation of Antichrist as the great idolater, and the persecutor of God's people. That is to say—it will be only *three years and a half at most* before the Lord's descent upon the Earth. But we must dwell upon this stroke of desolation for an instant.

In the *fourteenth chapter* of the REVELATION, we find—"the first fruits unto God and to the Lamb" brought before us assembled together with Christ "on Mount Zion, and following Him whithersoever He goeth." Then we have the word of exhortation uttered by an angel's voice to every nation, and kindred and tongue and people, "fear God, and give glory to Him, for the hour of His judgment is come," which we have before alluded to as having probable reference to *a great revival of religion* following immediately upon the removal of the Lord's people from the Earth.* And now, in the next verse, we find the statement—"and there followed another angel, saying, BABYLON IS FALLEN, IS FALLEN, THAT GREAT CITY, BECAUSE SHE MADE ALL NATIONS DRINK OF THE WINE OF THE WRATH OF HER FORNICATION."

* See Chapter II.

And now again *another* angel follows, saying with a loud voice,—"If any man worship the beast and his image, and receive his mark in his forehead or in his hand, the same shall drink of the wine of the wrath of God." The proclamation concerning the fall of Babylon, coming, as it does, *after* the intimations of the first resurrection and the revival of religion,—and *before* the solemn warning respecting the beast and his image; it would appear, that although the overthrow of the great City will take place at the *beginning* of Antichrist's reign, it will be *before,* or *immediately upon,* this full development of his true character; and about synchronize with the commencement of Israel's great tribulation. But let us refer to another chapter which affords us more exact particulars about this overthrow; namely, the *eighteenth.* In this chapter we find a warning voice from Heaven—"come out of her (*i. e.* Babylon) my people, that ye be not partakers of her sins, and that ye receive not of her plagues . . . . her plagues shall come in one day, death, and mourning, and famine; and she shall be utterly burned with fire; for strong is the Lord God who judgeth her . . . . *in one hour* is thy judgment come. . . . . Rejoice over her, thou heaven, and ye holy apostles and prophets; for God hath avenged you on her. And a mighty angel took up a stone like a great millstone, and cast it into the sea, saying, thus with violence shall that great city Babylon be thrown down, and shall be found no more at all . . . . and in her was found the blood of prophets, and of saints, and of all that were slain upon the Earth." So does the word of prophecy foretell the sudden and entire overthrow of "Babylon the Great," which we have shown beyond all doubt is ROME.* Whether by what is said, we are to understand that ROME,—THE ACTUAL CITY, will be suddenly destroyed by fire; or whether the iniquitous POWER OF THE PAPACY which has its rule in this City as its great centre, is referred to, is not perhaps quite clear. But I think there is sufficient evidence to show plainly that the destruction of the *actual City* is intended; for, if we refer to the account given us of the overthrow of *the Papacy*, in the *seventeenth chapter*,† we find that the overthrow of the "City," in the light of *a power "which reigneth over the Kings of the Earth,"* will be a *gradual* work, brought about by the hatred of Antichrist and his ten kings; whereas *this* destruction is to be *sudden*,—the work of "*one hour*,"—and *the Kings of the Earth* who were brought before us as the DESTROYERS in the *former* case, are declared in *this latter* to BEWAIL her, and LAMENT for her, when they see the smoke of her burning.‡ Surely, moreover, there was a fulness of meaning, when the "mighty angel took up a stone like a great millstone, and cast it into the sea, saying, thus *with violence* shall that great city Babylon be thrown down, and shall be found no more at all. And the voice of harpers and musicians shall be heard no more at all in thee; and no craftsmen, of whatsoever craft he be, shall be found any more in thee . . . . and the light of a candle shall shine no more at all in thee; and the voice of the bridegroom and of the bride shall be heard no more at all in

* See Chapter III.   † Verses 15—18.   ‡ Rev. xviii. 9, 10.

thee." Reason would that we should conclude *almost positively*, since we have such a word as this, that when, through the hatred of Antichrist and his ten kings, the *Papal power* shall have been overthrown; —the Lord Himself will take the judgment of the CITY into His own hand and *with a flood of fire* DESTROY IT UTTERLY.

But now this work of judgment on THE CITY OF SUCH BITTER PERSECUTIONS AND EXCEEDING WRONGS, will not pass unobserved by those who are IN HEAVEN. The risen saints with Christ behold, and utter praise immediately. For mark how the next chapter opens—"And after these things, I heard a great voice of much people in Heaven, saying, Alleluia; salvation and glory, and honor, and power, unto the Lord our God; for true and righteous are his judgments; for He hath judged the great whore, which did corrupt the earth with her fornication, and hath avenged the blood of His servants at her hand. And again they said Alleluia; and her smoke rose up forever and ever."*

But they have more to witness yet ere they descend from the expanse above, with the Almighty Judge, to earth. There must be *more judgments on the wicked;* and *the last great tribulation of the Church* and *Israel must receive the completion of their measure*, that their cup of sorrow may be filled unto repentance.

Thus, then, *when* the great Harlot City Babylon is fallen, and the warning voice is uttered by the angel, "If any man worship the beast or his image

---

* Rev. xix. 1—8.

.... he shall drink of the wine of the wrath of God .... and .... be tormented with fire and brimstone in the presence of the holy angels, and in the presence of the Lamb;" *then* the Saints who yet adorn the earth are spoken of: for the day of their "patience" has come. A voice is heard from Heaven, bidding the Apostle "write—Blessed are the dead which die in the Lord from henceforth: yea, saith the Spirit, that they may rest from their labors, and their works do follow them."* And now we have the Lord, "the Son of Man" *enthroned upon a white cloud, prepared to reap and gather the abundant harvest.* A persecution unto death, which has not known a precedent, shall cut down its thousands, who will be added to the shining throngs above, till the whole earth is reaped and the whole harvest gathered. Thus the "great multitude, which no man could number, out of all nations, and kindreds, and people, and tongues,"† are prepared to stand before the Throne of God and of the Lamb. They "have come out of great tribulation (ἐκ τῆς θλίψεως τῆς μεγάλης, out of *the* tribulation *the great one*) and shall be before the Throne forever. But when the whole number is completed; all the subjects of the Saviour's kingdom gathered; and no faith remains upon the earth; then the "voice from the throne" is heard, saying, "Praise our God all ye His servants, and ye that fear Him, both small and great." And the Apostle adds, "I heard as it were the voice of a great multitude, and as the voice of many waters, and as the voice of mighty thundering, saying, Alleluia; for the Lord

* *Rev. xiv. 12, 13.*   † *Rev. vii. 9—17.*

God omnipotent reigneth. Let us be glad and rejoice, and give honor to Him: for the marriage of
the Lamb is come, and his wife hath made herself
ready."* And now the whole Church,—the bride
of Christ,—appears, arrayed in fine linen, clean and
white: no member wanting: no trembling, weak disciple left unheeded. *All* who have believed in Jesus
Christ are found among the blissful throng, and all
rejoice exceedingly, for the last tribulation of the
Church is finished, and, for joy, it is to be no more
remembered by the sainted sufferers. But on the
earth, as we learn from our Redeemer's words, *great
signs and wonders are beheld.* The sun is darkened,
the moon does not give her light, the stars fall from
heaven, and the powers of heaven are shaken. Let
me remark here that these signs in heaven are nowhere spoken of as taking place till "*After*" *the last
great tribulation.* In MATTHEW the language upon
this is very plain,—"*Immediately* AFTER *the tribulation of those days* shall the sun be darkened, and the
moon shall not give her light, and the stars shall fall
from heaven, and the powers of heaven shall be
shaken, and *then*," it is added, "shall appear the
sign of the Son of Man in heaven."† The language
of ST. MARK speaks plainly also.—"But in those
days, *after* that tribulation, the sun shall be darkened, and the moon shall not give her light, and the
stars of heaven shall fall, and the powers that are in
heaven shall be shaken. And then shall they see
the Son of Man coming in the clouds."‡ In ST.
LUKE we find the exact period for these wonders to

---

* Rev. xix. 6, 7.   † Matt. xxiv. 29, 30.   ‡ Mark xiii. 24—26.

be that in which the completion of "the times of the Gentiles" shall be arrived at. He informs us that the same remarkable instances as those which are mentioned both by MATTHEW and MARK will come to pass; but with *these* additions,—"upon the Earth distress of nations with perplexity; the sea and the waves roaring; men's hearts failing them for fear, and for looking after those things which are coming on the earth.*

At the time, then, WHEN THE TRIBULATION SHALL HAVE DONE ITS WORST AGAINST GOD'S PEOPLE, shall these signs and wonders be revealed.

But in that day, it is clear, that though the hand of *persecution* will be staid for want of saints to persecute,—the hand of *cruelty and bloodshed* will be lifted up with power. Upon the earth will be "*distress of nations with perplexity.*"

But further, it is evident that JERUSALEM WILL BE THE CENTRE OF THE FEARFUL WARFARE. *There will* Antichrist "plant the tabernacle of his palace." *There* will be THE SEAT OF THE LAST STRUGGLE BETWEEN ALL THE POWERS OF EARTH. Against that Holy City will all nations of the earth be gathered to "THE BATTLE OF THE GREAT DAY OF GOD ALMIGHTY."

Important details with regard to this are found in the Prophet DANIEL. He brings before us the last king—the Antichrist—having his seat in Palestine, and *dividing the land "for gain."* He then tells us how that "at the time of the end, the King of the South shall push at him, and the King of the North

* Luke xxi. 24—27.

shall come against him like a whirlwind . . . . and tidings out of the east and out of the north shall trouble him;" wherefore "he shall go forth with great fury to destroy and utterly to make away many. *And he shall plant the tabernacle of his palace between the seas in the Glorious Holy mountain."**

JOEL follows in the same direction,—speaking of the troubles of that time when "the day of the Lord cometh . . . . . and is nigh at hand," the day when "the earth shall quake . . . . the heavens shall tremble, the sun and the moon shall be dark, and the stars shall withdraw their shining," declares that "in those days" . . . . the Lord "will gather all nations, and will bring them down to the *valley of Jehoshaphat*, and plead with them there." . . . . "Proclaim ye this (he says) among the Gentiles,— prepare war, wake up the mighty men . . . . beat your plowshares into swords, and your pruning hooks into spears: let the weak say, I am strong. Assemble yourselves and come all ye heathen, and gather yourselves together round about: *thither* cause thy mighty ones to come down O Lord. Let the heathen be awakened, and come up to the *valley of Jehoshaphat:* for *there* will I sit to judge all the heathen round about. . . . . Multitudes, multitudes in the valley of decision: for the day of the Lord is near in the valley of decision. The sun and the moon shall be darkened, and the stars shall withdraw their shining."

ZECHARIAH likewise testifies, "Behold *I will make*

---

* Daniel xi. 39—45.

Jerusalem a cup of trembling unto all the people round about, when they shall be in the siege both *against Judah, and against Jerusalem.* And in that day, *I will make Jerusalem a burdensome stone for all people;* all that burden themselves with it shall be cut in pieces, though all the people of the earth be gathered together against it. . . . . Behold the day of the Lord cometh and thy spoil shall be divided in the midst of thee. For *I will gather all nations against Jerusalem to battle;* and the City shall be taken . . . . and half of the City shall go forth into Captivity, and the residue of the people shall not be cut off from the City. Then shall the Lord go forth . . . . *and His feet shall stand in that day upon the Mount of Olives, which is before Jerusalem on the east* . . . . and the Lord my God shall come, and all the Saints."*

THUS JERUSALEM SHALL BE THE GRAND CENTRE OF THE EARTH'S AFFLICTION WHEN THE DAY OF THE LORD'S COMING IS AT HAND.

Now perhaps it may have surprised some persons that I have not referred to the (so-called) "BATTLE OF ARMAGEDDON," while speaking of the final acts of warfare near Jerusalem. Let me say a word in explanation of this omission.

I may, in the first place, state plainly that I do not think that we are right in making the assertion that a battle *properly so called* will take place. If we look at the *sixteenth chapter* of REVELATION, which is the only place in the whole Bible in which ARMAGEDDON is brought before us, we shall not find

* Zech. xii. 2—4. xxv.—15.

that a *Battle* of Armageddon is spoken of, but simply A GATHERING TOGETHER OF THE KINGS OF THE EARTH, *through the instrumentality of evil spirits*, at a place called ARMAGEDDON, in readiness for "THE BATTLE OF THE GREAT DAY OF GOD ALMIGHTY;" which battle—as we have already seen—is to be fought *in the immediate neighborhood of* JERUSALEM.

Now surely it will not be argued that JERUSALEM was spoken of as "a place called in the *Hebrew tongue*—ARMAGEDDON:" for *"Jerusalem"* is itself a *Hebrew* name. Some other place than this, must be intended.* A *gathering* however at *some* place so called if rendered in the Hebrew tongue there will be. It will be, no doubt, a congress of kings, held at the place, to decide on matters with regard to Eastern territories,—matters of importance to the nations generally. It will be a congress called by *Antichrist* in subtlety, so that by the semblance of peace, many may be destroyed. It would appear that this congress will be held soon after "the first resurrection" (of which we have spoken at large)† shall have taken place. So at least, the language of the chapter which contains the notice of the gathering, would lead us to expect. For we find that as

---

* There are different opinions as to the etymology of Armageddon. Some suppose it to be composed of the two words עֵר a city, and מִגְד something very noble. Others tell us, it should be חַר a mountain, and מִגְד. Others again that it is either עֵר or חַר and מִגְדּוֹ Megiddo. Of this last word we may note that the Septuagint renders it Μαγεδδω. Gesenius suggests that Meggido may mean "a place of crowds."

† See Chapter II.

soon as it is said—"I saw three unclean spirits like frogs, come out of the mouth of the dragon, and out of the mouth of the beast, and out of the mouth of the false prophet; for they are the spirits of devils, working miracles, which go forth unto the kings of the earth and of the whole world, to gather them to the battle of the great day of God Almighty:"—a word of solemn warning follows,— *"Behold, I come as a thief. Blessed is he that watcheth and keepeth his garments, lest he walk naked and they see his shame."*

This warning being uttered—the prophetic history proceeds,—"And he gathered them together into a place called in the Hebrew tongue Armageddon."

Then immediately "the seventh vial is poured into the air," and the voice from heaven—from the temple, and from the throne declares—"IT IS DONE." Now signs and wonders follow. Babylon receives her cup of wrath. The islands and the mountains flee away. And men's hearts failing them for fear, and their bodies suffering from the plague of hail, they *blaspheme God.*

Another subject of general inquiry, because thought to be of serious moment as a sign of the approach of Christ for judgment, is the PROPHESYING OF THE WITNESSES. On this also I have said nothing.

Now there can be no doubt that previous to the advent of our Lord, THE PROPHET ELIJAH will appear on earth.

That he has *not come yet, is certain. John the Baptist was not* ELIJAH. He *said* he was not. "I

8

not Elias" was his reply to those who asked him.*
ar Lord indeed declared of him "this is Elias
hich was for to come."† And so indeed he was.
e was Elias as to "the *power* and *spirit*;"‡ the
Elias (so to speak) who was to be the herald of the
Saviour's *peaceful* mission. But he was *not* Elias—
in person—not the *actual* Elijah who was taken up
to Heaven in the fiery chariot. It was nowhere said
he *was* to come before the *first*,—the *peaceful*—day
of the Lord Jesus;—but as Malachi predicted—
"*before the coming of the* GREAT AND DREADFUL *day
of the Lord*," the day when He shall come for judgment and to take possession of His kingdom. No
doubt Elijah, therefore, has *not yet appeared*, but
IS TO COME. But *where is the evidence that he is to*
be one of the "TWO WITNESSES?" We cannot find it.
If we refer to the *Eleventh Chapter of* REVELATION,
we shall see, I think, that the "TWO WITNESSES" are
introduced, not under the *last*, but under the SIXTH
trumpet. This trumpet *does not speak of* THE LORD'S
ADVENT. It is the trumpet of the *Reformation
period*.§ It is *not* the trumpet which proclaims THE
END. Therefore, these Witnesses *must have appeared
already*, unless the trumpet of the Reformation period
has not ceased to sound. But no fair interpreter of
the Apocalypse will maintain this, unless indeed h
assert likewise, that ALL the symbols of the Revel
tion are yet future as to their fulfilment; whi
notion *we* cannot for a moment think to be correct
There can be no doubt from the manner

* John i. 21. † Matt. ii. 14. ‡ Luke i.
§ Commencing probably at or about A.D. 1517, See Chapter

position of the narration, that the slaughter of the witnesses and their resurrection, together with the earthquake and the fall of the Tenth part of the City, were to be the terminating events under this trumpet. Now a careful examination of the details of the *seventh* trumpet, which are given in REVELATION, from the *fifteenth verse* of the *eleventh* to the *end* of the *nineteenth chapters*, will, I think show us the extreme probability that the *sixth* trumpet ceased to sound upon the rise of the Napoleon dynasty. If so, I feel no] hesitation whatever in asserting the opinion that the TWO WITNESSES, are none other than THE PROPHETS AND THE APOSTLES GENERALLY; or in other words, THE OLD AND NEW TESTAMENT SCRIPTURES; for it is certain that these inspired witnesses of God did prophesy, as it were, clothed in sackcloth, for *twelve hundred and sixty years;* namely from 533 A.D. (when the EDICT OF JUSTINIAN planted the nucleus of that persecuting power of the Papacy which it swayed with such effect in after years) till the REIGN OF TERROR, 1793, when so far as their existence in the Roman Empire was concerned, *they were slain;* and thus for *three and a half years* (the time predicted) viz., from the 31*st of May*, 1793 (when, by the success of the Jacobin Conspirators, the destruction of the civil establishment of religion in France was completed, the "*Worship of Reason*" commenced, the *Scriptures were declared to be a fable*, death was pronounced an everlasting sleep, the Sabbath was abolished, and the reckoning of time altered), to the beginning of the year, 1797, (when a change took place by the fact of new men obtaining power in the great council of the Commonwealth.)

During this predicted period, it was as the prophecy declared it should be: (verse 10). Joy was exhibited amongst the learned and scientific people of all Europe. They wrote one to another, offering congratulations on the introduction of a new era. Our own beloved country was infected also, and Republicanism and infidelity committed ravages on every side.

But now for a moment we must glance again at Earth. "THE SIGN OF THE SON OF MAN" has appeared in Heaven, in the sight of the wicked world. "The sign" (το σημεῖον), some evidence, some clear intimation, which men cannot gainsay. *It appears;* and the tribes of the earth mourn.* The heaven departs "as a scroll when it is rolled together:" and reveals the *wondrous truth.* THE DESPISED JESUS AND HIS ONCE PERSECUTED PEOPLE ARE DESCENDING. "Every mountain and island are moved out of their places. And the Kings of the earth, and the great men, and the rich men, and the chief captains, and the mighty men, and every bondman, and every freeman, hide themselves in the dens and in the rocks of the mountains; and say to the mountains and rocks, fall on us, and hide us from the face of Him that sitteth on the throne, and from the wrath of the Lamb; for the great day of His wrath is come, and who shall be able to stand."† But he descends. *"This same Jesus" who was seen to go into heaven, so descends in like manner as He was seen to go into heaven.*‡

* Matt. xxiv. 30. † Rev. vi. 14—17. ‡ Acts. i. 2.

And, as ZECHARIAH tells us, He stands upon the Mount of Olives, and the mountain cleaves in the midst thereof towards the east and towards the west: and half of the mountain removes towards the north, and half of it towards the south.*

Thus indeed it shall be. Standing on that very Mount of Olives—where in time gone by He rode meekly on an Ass's Colt,—THE KING OF KINGS SHALL MANIFEST HIMSELF. We need not add any words to make this clearer or more positive than it is made by Holy Scripture.

* Zech. xiv. 4.

CHAPTER V.

THE JUDGMENT OF THE NATIONS.

"In righteousness He doth judge and make war."—Rev. xix. 11.

Religious people often speak of "THE LAST DAY,"—or—"THE DAY OF THE LORD,"—or "THE DAY OF JUDGMENT," as if it were to be a day of ordinary duration, to come suddenly upon the world: A certain day of twelve or four and twenty hours, appointed by the Father, in which a complete destruction of all sublunary, if not heavenly, things, is to take place; and the righteous and the wicked, being raised and judged, rewards and punishments of everlasting nature are to be awarded them.*

The present chapter will be occupied with the consideration of those great events which will peculiarly mark the MORNING of this "Last Day." I have included these events, when mentioning "the general order" of the subjects which would occupy these chapters, under the title of "THE JUDGMENT OF THE NATIONS."†

The terms in which the PROPHETS speak of this great judgment is exceedingly impressive. . . . . Their language points to it as one of the greatest among great events. The world is represented to be full of

* Chapter I., page 20, 21.   † See Chapter I., page 20.

wickedness; the hand of cruelty uplifted high; the thoughts of all men far from Him in whose hand is their life, their breath, and all things. But suddenly a stop is put upon their rashness. The Lord descends. He comes with all His Saints. He comes in righteousness to judge and make war: He comes prepared to avenge the blood of all His servants who have fallen by the hand of wickedness: He comes in readiness to vindicate His honor in the sight of the ungodly, and to take possession of the throne which appertains to Him as "KING OF KINGS AND LORD OF LORDS."

But let us observe the testimony which these prophets offer.

ISAIAH tells us—in his *second chapter*, that "It shall come to pass in the last days, that the mountain of the Lord's house shall be established in the top of the mountains, and shall be exalted above the hills; and all nations shall flow unto it. And many people shall go and say, come ye, and let us go up to the mountain of the Lord, to the house of the God of Jacob: and He will teach us of His ways, and we will walk in His paths: for out of Zion shall go forth the law, and the word of the Lord from Jerusalem. Here we have certainly a very glorious time foretold: a time yet future, such as has not hitherto appeared. Other quotations from the prophet Isaiah need not be given, as his whole prophecy is full of similar testimonies.

JOEL speaks very plainly on the subject. In the *third chapter*,—to which reference was made in the last chapter with regard to the gathering of all nations against Jerusalem, we read—"Behold in those days, when I bring again the captivity of Judah and Jerusalem, I will also gather all nations, and will bring them down to the valley of Jehoshaphat and will plead with them there. . . . . Let the heathen come up to the valley of Jehoshaphat, *for there will I sit to judge all the heathen round about.* . . . . Multitudes, multitudes in the Valley of Decision; for the DAY OF THE LORD is near, in the Valley of Decision. The sun and the moon shall be darkened, and the stars shall withdraw their shining." Surely so far as this passage affords information, "he who runs may read" what God will do when He shall appear on the behalf of Israel. He will "*plead with,*"—He will "*judge*"—the nations. The *valley of Jehoshaphat* will be the place of judgment,—there He will sit and execute the fierceness of His anger, while the sun and the moon shall become dark, and the stars shall withdraw their shining. Now this act of judgment will be preparatory to the establishment of Israel in the full possession of their land:—for we are told,—immediately after this declaration of judgment and terror is made,—that "The Lord also shall roar out of ZION, and utter His voice from JERUSALEM; and the heavens and the earth shall shake: but the Lord will be the hope of His people, and the strength of the children of Israel. So shall ye know that I am the Lord your God, dwelling in Zion, my holy mountain: then shall Jerusalem be holy, and there shall no strangers pass through her any more. And it shall come to pass in that day, that the mountains shall drop down new wine, and the hills shall flow with milk, and .... Judah shall dwell for ever, and Jerusalem from generation to generation. For I will cleanse their blood that I have not cleansed: for the Lord dwelleth in Zion." How evident it is then, that the great act of judgment upon the nations shall *precede* and *immediately introduce* the happy reign of Israel's peace.

But again. We will consider what ZEPHANIAH was commissioned to declare. In the *third chapter* we find the Lord speaking by his servant, thus:—"My determination is to gather the NATIONS, that I may assemble the KINGDOMS, to pour upon them mine indignation, even all my fierce anger; for all the earth shall be devoured with the fire of my jealousy." And now let us mark what follows—"Then will I return to the people a pure language, that they may all call upon the name of the Lord, to serve him with one consent..... The remnant of Israel shall do no iniquity nor speak lies; neither shall a deceitful tongue be found in their mouth: for they shall feed, and lie down, and none shall make them afraid..... The King of Israel, even the Lord, is in the midst of thee: thou shalt not see evil any more." Here too, then, the same lesson is advanced.

And so likewise in the Prophet ZECHARIAH. The *tenth, eleventh, twelfth, and thirteenth* chapters speak of ISRAEL *first* RESTORED IN UNBELIEF under the auspices of "THE IDOL SHEPHERD;" *then* BESEIGED BY ALL NATIONS; and *at last*, DRIVEN TO A BITTER MOURNING FOR THEIR SINS, AND A TRUE-HEARTED RETURN TO GOD IN CHRIST. The *fourteenth chapter* retraces a little, and gives valuable explanation. It says—"Behold the day of the Lord cometh, and thy spoil shall be divided in the midst of thee. For I will gather all nations against Jerusalem to battle; and the city shall be taken, and the houses rifled, and the women ravished; and half of the city shall go forth into captivity, and the residue of the people shall not be cut off from the city." This will be the sign of the immediate Advent, for it is added "THEN SHALL THE LORD GO FORTH, and fight against those nations, as when He fought in the day of battle. And His feet shall stand in that day upon the Mount ⸱of Olives, which is before Jerusalem on the east; and the Mount of Olives shall cleave in the midst thereof, towards the east and towards the west, and there shall be a very great valley; and half of the mountain shall remove toward the north, and half of it toward the south. And ye shall flee to the valley of the mountains; for the valley of the mountains shall reach unto Azal; yea, ye shall flee, like as ye fled from before the earthquake in the days of Uzziah, king of Judah: AND THE LORD MY GOD SHALL COME, AND ALL THE SAINTS WITH THEE . . . . and the Lord shall be king over all the earth . . . . and there shall be no more utter destruction; but Jerusalem shall be safely inhabited."

So then, we are left without a doubt, that when the Lord shall come again upon our earth, it will be to perform *at once* an act of FEARFUL JUDGMENT ON THE NATIONS. And we are prepared to understand the declaration of St. JOHN which is made in the *nineteenth chapter* of the REVELATION, where the descent of Him who bears the title "King of Kings and Lord of Lords" is spoken of—"And I saw an angel standing in the sun: and he cried with a loud voice, saying to all the fowls that fly in the midst of heaven, Come and gather yourselves together to the supper of the Great God; that ye may eat the flesh of kings, and the flesh of captains, and the flesh of mighty men, and the flesh of horses, and of them that sit on them, and the flesh of all men, both free and bond, both small and great."

But while we speak of the Lord's judgment of the wicked nations, we must not omit to notice the peculiar stress which is laid, both in the OLD and NEW Testaments, upon the heavy stroke of Judgment which shall fall on him who shall have been THE LEADER, first of ISRAEL to the re-possession of their land, and then of ALL THE NATIONS of the earth, in seige against their tribes.

In the *tenth chapter* of ISAIAH we read of "the Assyrian:"—probably the ancient dynasty of Assyrian monarchs and their works of power, as God's instrument for the punishment of Israel. But in the *twelfth verse* we find the following prediction;—"It shall come to pass, that, when the Lord *hath performed His* WHOLE *work upon Mount Zion and on Jerusalem*, I will punish THE FRUIT of the stout heart of the King of Assyria, and the glory of his high looks. For he saith, by the strength of my hand I have done it, and by my wisdom; for I am prudent; and I have removed the bounds of the people, and have robbed their treasures, and I have put down the inhabitants like a valiant man; and my hand hath found, as a nest, the riches of the people.

. . . . O my people that dwelleth in Zion, be not afraid of the Assyrian; . . . . for yet a very little while, and the indignation shall cease, and mine anger *in their destruction.* And the Lord of Hosts shall stir up a scourge for him, according to the slaughter of Midian at the rock of Oreb. . . . . And it shall come to pass in that day, that his burden shall be taken from off thy shoulder, and his yoke from off thy neck, and the yoke shall be destroyed, because of the anointing. . . . . He shall shake his hand against the Mount of the daughter of Zion, the Hill of Jerusalem. Behold, the Lord, *the Lord of Hosts shall lop the bough with terror,* and the high ones of stature shall be hewn down, and the haughty ones shall be humbled." And immediately upon this prophecy of the Assyrian's destruction, the "ROD OUT OF THE STEM OF JESSE" is brought before us, and the reign of righteousness and peace is introduced. But let us refer to the *fourteenth chapter* of this Prophet. In the account he there gives us of the events which shall take place at the destruction of the mysterious Babylon of the latter days, he tells us that the last king thereof—"THE ASSYRIAN"— shall meet with his End IN THE LAND OF ISRAEL. "I will break the Assyrian— (saith the Lord) *in my land, and upon my mountains.*

Again in DANIEL—the *eleventh chapter,* in which the same last king of the last empire is evidently spoken of;* we read that "He shall plant the tabernacles of his palace between the seas in the glorious holy mountain; yet he shall come to his end, and

* See Chapter III.

none shall help him. And at that time shall Michael stand up: the great prince which standeth for the children of thy people."

The same fact is implied in the language of St. Paul, where he declares—that *the Lord will consume that wicked one with the spirit of His mouth, and destroy Him with the brightness of His coming.*[*] For this is tantamount to saying that *at* or *near* the very place where the man Christ Jesus shall appear, namely in the land of Israel,—the stroke of judgment will descend upon the head of Antichrist.

So, then, upon the repeated word of Scripture, we conclude that Antichrist will receive his portion of the Lord's first act of judgment, IN THE LAND OF ISRAEL.

But these passages and others show us likewise what *the express judgment* shall be which this WICKED ONE shall receive.

In the *fourteenth chapter* of ISAIAH, we find that he shall be "cut down to the ground . . . . brought down to the grave . . . . TO HELL, TO THE SIDES OF THE PIT, cast out of the grave like an abominable branch." In the *thirtieth chapter*, which speaks of the same terminal period and the same events which are elsewhere brought forward as the characteristic marks of "the last time,"—we find the Prophet speaking thus—"The Lord shall cause his glorious voice to be heard, and shall show the lighting down of His arm, with the indignation of his anger, and with the flame of a devouring fire, with scattering, and tempest, and hailstones. For through the voice

* 2 Thess: ii. 3.

of the Lord shall THE ASSYRIAN be beaten down, which smote with a rod. For TOPHET is ordained of old; yea, FOR THE KING it is prepared: He hath made it deep and large; the pile thereof is fire and much wood: the breath of the Lord, like a stream of brimstone, doth kindle it."

Thus we find that the judgment of "the Assyrian" will be a judgment of severity. He will be "brought down to hell,"—being "beaten down" by "the voice of the Lord," and he will be consigned to the fire of "Tophet."

DANIEL speaks very clearly with reference to the manner in which the FOURTH (or ROMAN) EMPIRE shall be overthrown: but of "THE LITTLE HORN"— THE ANTICHRIST—which arises out of that Empire, *the fact* of his destruction *only* is declared. Of the EMPIRE it is said,—"I beheld even till the beast was slain, and his body destroyed, and given to the burning flame."[*] But of the HORN, the last king thereof, —the Antichrist;—it is said—"He shall be broken without hand."[†] The wrath "determined shall be poured upon" him.[‡] "He shall come to his end, and none shall help him."[§]

We have referred already to the word of PAUL upon the subject,—"Then shall that wicked be revealed, whom the Lord shall consume with the spirit of His mouth, and destroy with the brightness of His coming."[||] But let us observe how closely this agrees with that which was advanced by ISAIAH and Daniel. *The "voice" of the Lord,—"the breath*

---

[*] Daniel vii. 11.   [†] Daniel viii. 25.   [‡] Daniel ix. 27.
[§] Daniel xi. 45.   [||] 2 Thess. ii. 8.

of the Lord like a stream of brimstone,"—"the spirit of His mouth,"—is the instrument; and the destruction takes place *"without hand,"* but *"with the flame of a devouring fire,"—"with the brightness of His coming."*

But let us make one more reference. In the *nineteenth chapter* of REVELATION, which speaks particularly of the Advent of our Lord with His Saints; we find the Apostle John declaring,—"And I saw the beast, and the kings of the earth, and their armies, gathered together to make war against Him that sat upon the horse, (that is "the King of Kings,") and against His army. And THE BEAST was taken, and with him the FALSE PROPHET, *that wrought miracles before him*, with which he deceived them that had received the mark of the beast, and them that worshipped his image. THESE BOTH WERE CAST ALIVE INTO A LAKE OF FIRE, BURNING WITH BRIMSTONE. And the remnant were slain with the sword of Him that sat upon the horse, which sword proceeded out of His mouth."

This is the most *detailed* account of Antichrist's destruction which is given us. And here we find again entire agreement with the assertions which have preceded.

So, then, *in the Holy Land, at the Advent of the Lord, by the breath of His mouth, with the brightness of His coming*, SHALL ANTICHRIST MEET HIS DESTRUCTION. He shall be taken *with the False Prophet*, and "be cast alive into *the lake of fire;*" the *"Tophet"* which was ordained of old and prepared *"for the king."* Thus shall these two workers of iniquity have their portion in the lake of fire and brimstone, *before others, even before Satan himself,*—for the *twentieth chapter* of REVELATION teaches us that Satan will abide for yet a *thousand years* before he shall be cast into this lake, because there is a final stroke of wickedness which he must be reserved to execute, to the great end that sin may be *forever* overthrown: and then, it is declared, "the devil that deceiveth" the nations shall be "cast into the lake of fire and brimstone, where the beast and the false prophet are, and shall be tormented day and night for ever and ever." But of this we have to speak in a future chapter.

We have mentioned "THE FALSE PROPHET," as the companion of the Antichrist. His bosom friend, it would appear: his counsellor, his priest; the one by whom he is to work his miracles. Expounders of Prophecy have varied much in their ideas respecting this person. Some have spoken of him very confidently as the last Bishop of Rome, but having his seat transferred to *Jerusalem,* and there, taking part with Antichrist in denying both the Father and the Son,* and in establishing idolatry. Others, that this *false prophet* will be some individual, holding, or pretending to hold, an intimate communication with spiritual existences. Others again have held notions of a kind very different from these; considering him, as they consider Antichrist, to be, not an individual, but *an apostate Church* or an *infidel system,* having great pretensions.

It will be readily conceived, from the general tone

* 1 John ii. 22.

of these chapters, that I believe the FALSE PROPHET will be a PERSON. But whether he will have an episcopal or papal title, or whether he will be an infidel necromancer, I do not find so far revealed, that any fair hypothesis can be formed concerning it. The day of Antichrist will show the world quite soon enough concerning such a wicked one.

And now, when these great powers of evil shall have been consigned to their own place, and the remnant of the workers of iniquity shall have been "slain with the sword of Him that sitteth upon the horse,"* the world will have assumed a fearful aspect truly. But few men will be left, while multitudes from all the nations will be slain upon the surface of the earth. "There shall be as the shaking of an olive tree, and as the gleaning grapes when the vintage is done,"† *and no more:* "A very small remnant" left to Israel, and a few found here and there among the Gentiles. *These only* will be left upon the earth. That such a remnant *will* be left, is evident, for the word of God has plainly declared it.

See for example what ISAIAH says in the *tenth chapter*, where he speaks, as we have shown already, of the destruction of Antichrist and the ungodly nations. "Therefore shall the Lord, the Lord of Hosts, send among his fat ones leanness; and under His glory He shall kindle a burning, like the burning of a fire . . . . and it shall consume the glory of His forest, and of His fruitful field, *both soul and body:* and they shall be as when a standard-bearer fainteth. *And the rest of the trees of the forest shall*

* Rev. xix. 21.   † Isaiah xxiv.

9

be few, that a child may write them. And it shall come to pass in that day that the REMNANT OF ISRAEL, and such as are escaped of the house of Judah, shall stay upon the Lord, the Holy One of Israel, in truth. *The remnant shall return, even the remnant of Jacob, unto the mighty God.**

We find the Prophet JEREMIAH also in his *thirtieth chapter* speaking by the word of God to Israel, "though I make a full end of all nations whither I have scattered thee, *yet will I not make a full end of thee:* but I will correct thee in measure, and will not leave thee altogether unpunished.

JOEL foretells plainly in the *second chapter* of the remnant which shall be spared in the last day, thus: "It shall come to pass, that whosoever shall call on the name of the Lord shall be delivered: for in Mount Zion and in Jerusalem shall be deliverance, as the Lord hath said, and in the remnant whom the Lord shall call."†

God also speaks by ZECHARIAH in the *thirteenth chapter*, saying,—"I will bring *the third part* through the fire, and will refine them as silver is refined, and will try them as gold is tried; they shall call on my name, and I will hear them; I will say, It is my people; and they shall say, The Lord is my God."‡

Of the Remnant of *Israel* which is chiefly brought before us in these passages, we are taught by JEREMIAH and ZECHARIAH,§ that they shall be brought to the Lord "with weeping and with supplications." That God "will pour upon the house of David and

---

* Isaiah x. 16—21.   † Joel ii. 32.   ‡ Zechariah xiii. 9.
§ Jeremiah xxxi. 8—25. Zechariah xii. 10—14.

the inhabitants of Jerusalem, the spirit of grace and of supplications; and they shall look on "Him whom they have pierced, and they shall mourn for Him, as one mourneth for his only son, and be a bitterness for Him, as one that is in bitterness for his first-born." Thus, therefore, *at the eleventh hour*, there shall be mercy for the remnant of Israel, "according to the election of grace." But also, there shall be a remnant from among the *Gentile* nations: for the Ensign is to be upreared for *them:* as it is written in the *eleventh chapter* of Isaiah,—"And in that day, (the day of the Redeemer's reign of peace) there shall be a root of Jesse, which shall stand up for an ensign *of the people;* to it shall the *Gentiles* seek; and His rest shall be glorious." So again in the *sixtieth chapter* we read "the *Gentiles* shall come to thy (Israel's) light, and kings to the brightness of thy rising . . . . the forces of the *Gentiles* shall come unto thee, ... surely the isles shall wait for me, and the ships of Tarshish first, to bring the sons from far . . . . unto the name of the Lord thy God, and to the Holy One of Israel, because He hath glorified thee. And the sons of strangers shall build up thy walls, and their kings shall minister unto thee. . . . . The *Sons* also of them that afflicted thee shall come bending unto thee: and all that despised thee, shall bow themselves down at the soles of thy feet; and they shall call thee, the city of the Lord, The Zion of the Holy One of Israel."* But how shall this be, unless a remnant of the Gentile nations shall be left? Doubtless, both of JEWS and GENTILES there will be many who *knew not* the

* Isaiah lx.

Lord's will, for lack of opportunity; many *afar off,
who have never heard Christ's fame nor seen His
glory;* many to whom His word has been a sealed
book; a multitude, moreover, there will be of those
whose *tender years of infancy* will hold them free
from meriting the scourge of judgment when the rebel
nations meet their doom.

Thus will a vast multitude be gathered to re-people
all the earth, and bow submissively beneath the
righteous sceptre of the King of kings.

So far, we have looked upon the work of the first
act of judgment, *as it will affect the ranks of men.*
It remains now only that we note the *last* important
deed which is to mark the morning of the Lord's
Great Day—THE PUNISHMENT OF SATAN.

This ARCH-DECEIVER is not yet to be consigned to
the *eternal fire.* His work is not yet done.

Let us refer to the *twentieth chapter* of the REVE-
LATION, which commences thus:—"And I saw an
angel come down from Heaven, having the key of the
bottomless pit, and a great chain in his hand. And
he laid hold on the DRAGON that OLD SERPENT, which
is the DEVIL and SATAN; and BOUND HIM A
THOUSAND YEARS, and cast him into the BOT-
TOMLESS PIT, and shut him up, and set a seal upon
him, that he should deceive the nations no more, *till
the thousand years shall be fulfilled.*"

With such a word of Revelation we must be content. Explain we *cannot.* We dare not say that
this is allegory. But be it as it may, the lesson
it conveys is clear. The power of Satan will be
taken from him, so that he will tempt mankind no

longer for a season. He will no more walk as a roaring lion, to and fro, seeking whom he may devour. The trembling babe in Christ will have no longer need of fear because of him. No saint will be accused by him before the throne of God. He will be powerless towards mankind for the long period of "A THOUSAND YEARS."

So will the MORNING of the DAY OF CHRIST,—THE DAY OF JUDGMENT,—terminate. O what a morning it will be! What man can picture it! A morn replete with what is fearful for the child of this world,— glorious as the dawn of a bright day of joy unprecedented, for the child of grace. O blessed thought! The *weakest among those who now look up with faith to Jesus,* shall be delivered out of all the fear and woe which shall be poured from Heaven. He shall *behold* it all. The reeling earth, the raging sea, the madness of the people, shall he look upon; but with perfect confidence. He shall hear the wicked call upon the rocks to fall upon them, and the hills to cover them; he shall observe the wonders which shall make the heavens shake, but with a mind unruffled and devoid of fear; for with the rejoicing hosts of Jesus shall his place be found: amidst the shining throng which shall adorn the triumph of the Lord shall be his rest. With Christ, the King he shall descend from the high places of the saints' security. He shall descend, not to endure the bitter stroke of judgment, but *to judge;* to sit with the Great LORD OF LORDS upon the throne of the Millennial Kingdom; to be a KING, A PRIEST, A CO-HEIR WITH THE PRINCE OF PEACE AND GLORY.

My Brethren; IS IT WELL WITH YOU; that so you will not fail of safety in the awful ADVENT HOUR? That hour with which the dreadful morning of the JUDGMENT DAY shall dawn? Is it well with you NOW? Surely this is not a matter for delay. "*Now* is the accepted time." *To-morrow* may not be. O then suffer the plain question; ARE YOU NOW IN CHRIST? Have you yet gone to Him, *as a poor, helpless, worthless sinner*, and cast all your burden on His love and power to save? WHERE ARE YOUR SINS! Have you realized the fact that JESUS CHRIST has MADE ATONEMENT, full and perfect, for the utmost sin of EVERY BELIEVER? And have you taken all your sins believingly to Him, and trusted Him for pardon and salvation? If not, O think upon *His love*—His love which led Him to pour out His blood for your poor sin-bound soul, and trust *His Word* and rest on *His completed Work* which has been wrought that you might but BELIEVE and LIVE. Has He not written it in the unchanging records of His tender mercy, "HIM THAT COMETH UNTO ME, I WILL IN NO WISE CAST OUT."

CHAPTER VI.

THE REIGN OF PEACE.

"Behold a King shall reign in righteousness, and Princes shall rule in judgment."—Isaiah xxxii. 1.

WE have now to look upon the Tribulation of the "Latter Days," as *past;* the dominance of Iniquity, Bloodshed, and Perplexity, at an end: Antichrist consigned to the eternal flames; the Wicked of the earth destroyed; the Remnant brought to the acknowledgment of Christ as Lord and Saviour; Satan no longer able to deceive; and, visibly among mankind and angels, the self-same JESUS who was crucified, standing on the Mount of Olives, unopposed by any voice throughout the earth; and there establishing His right to reign as King of kings and Lord of lords. Thus will the Almighty God fulfil His ancient word against the reign of wickedness—"And thou profane wicked prince of Israel whose day is come, when iniquity shall have an end, Thus saith the Lord God, Remove the diadem, and take off the crown; this shall not be the same: exalt him that is low, and abase him that is high. I will overturn, overturn, overturn it; and it shall be no more, until He come, *whose right it is;* and I will give it him.* And thus

* Ezekiel xxi. 25—27.

the kingdom of the Lord of Hosts will come,—wherein His holy will shall be performed in earth as it is done in heaven.

This REIGN OF CHRIST,—the reign of RIGHT-EOUSNESS and PEACE, will form the subject of this chapter.

Among the Remnant of Israel—some inhabiting the Holy Land, and some dispersed among the Countries,—will no doubt be found a company from EVERY TRIBE. For God has promised that "He will be the God of ALL the families of Israel."* And so not only will MOUNT ZION rejoice, but MOUNT EPHRAIM also, as the Lord graciously declared by JEREMIAH in the *thirty-first chapter* of his prophecy,—"Behold I will bring them from the North country, and gather them from the coasts of the earth, ... a great company shall return thither. They shall come with weeping, and with supplications will I lead them: I will cause them to walk by the rivers of waters in a straight way, wherein they shall not stumble; for I am a Father to ISRAEL, and EPHRAIM is my first-born. Hear ye the Word of the Lord, O ye nations, and declare it in the Isles afar off, and say, He that scattered ISRAEL will gather him, and keep him as a shepherd doth his flock. . . . . Behold the days come, saith the Lord, that I will make a New Covenant *with the house of* ISRAEL *and with the house of* JUDAH."

So, too, did EZEKIEL prophesy in the *thirty-seventh chapter.* God had told him to take *two* sticks, and to "join them one to another into one stick," and

* Jeremiah xxxi. 1.

when the people should ask him what this meant, he was to answer them,—"Thus saith the Lord God, behold I will take the children of Israel from among the heathen whither they be gone, and will gather them on every side, and bring them into their own land: and I will make them ONE NATION in the land upon the mountains of Israel; and ONE KING shall be king to them all; and they shall be *no more two nations, neither shall they be divided into two kingdoms any more at all.*"

Thus then shall ALL THE TRIBES OF ISRAEL be gathered from among the countries, and brought safely to the land of their inheritance. And, as ISAIAH prophesied, the "ROOT OF JESSE .... shall stand for an ensign of the people .... and .... the Lord shall set His hand again the second time to recover the remnant of His people, which shall be left, from Assyria, and from Egypt, and from Pathros, and from Cush, and from Elam, and from Shinar, and from Hamath, and from the Islands of the Sea. And he shall set up an ensign for the nations, and shall assemble the outcasts of Israel, and gather together the dispersed of Judah from the four corners of the earth. The envy also of Ephraim shall depart, and the adversaries of Judah shall be cut off: Ephraim shall not envy Judah, and Judah shall not vex Ephraim."* The "ROOT OF JESSE" shall stand up to gather Israel His people;—not like the wicked Antichrist had *partly* gathered them *in unbelief*, but in the full assurance of a holy faith, and yet bewailing their rejection of the great Messiah.

* Isaiah xi. 10—13.

But let me add a word of explanation upon this.

Antichrist will be, as we have seen, *professedly* the friend of Israel, and under his protection *many* will be brought again to the possessions of their fore-fathers. But he will not bring *all Israel* back. It appears that he will only have to do with the tribes of JUDAH and BENJAMIN, and part of LEVI. If we refer to the Prophet ZECHARIAH, we shall find, in the *twelfth chapter*, a statement which will afford ground for this conclusion, which is not to be despised. He says,—"Jerusalem shall be inhabited again in her own place, even in Jerusalem. The Lord also shall save *the tents of Judah* FIRST, that the glory of the house of David and the glory of the inhabitants of Jerusalem do not magnify themselves against Judah. . . . . And I will pour upon the house of David, and upon the inhabitants of Jerusalem, the spirit of grace and of supplications; and they shall look upon Me whom they have pierced, and they shall mourn for Him, as one mourneth for his only son, and shall be in bitterness for Him, as one that is in bitterness for his first-born. In that day shall there be a great mourning in Jerusalem, as the mourning of Hada-drimmon in the valley of Megiddon. And the land shall mourn, every family apart; the family of the house of DAVID apart, and their wives apart; (here we have the representatives of the tribe of JUDAH:) the family of NATHAN apart, and their wives apart; (here, the representatives of the PROPHETS:) the family of the house of LEVI apart, and their wives apart; (here, the representatives of the tribe of LEVI and the PRIESTHOOD which pertained thereto:) the family of SHIMEI apart, and their wives apart; (here, the representatives of the tribe of Benjamin.*) ALL THE FAMILIES THAT REMAIN, every family apart, and their wives apart;" (here, the representatives, probably, of certain families of other tribes, which shall have returned and taken up their residence in Palestine, but shall not be found there in such numbers as to be worthy of especial note.) Now we know that the tribes of Israel, which at the present time inhabit those parts of the world with which Europeans and the western Asiatics have more especially to do, are necessarily (with a small exception, which is not easily discernible,) Judah, Benjamin, and Levi;—*the three tribes* which were taken captive by Nebuchadnezzar, restored under Zerubbabel, and dispersed under Titus. It is easy to understand the probability that *these* will be restored under THE LAST HEAD OF THE ROMAN EMPIRE—and that when at last the KING shall come "whose right it is to reign,"—He will take up the cause of Israel's tribes in all the earth, and will "set up an ensign for the nations," and "a sign among them, ... and they shall bring all" the "brethren of the house of Judah" "for an offering unto the Lord out of all nations, upon horses, and in chariots, and in litters, and upon mules, and upon swift beasts, to" God's "Holy Mountain Jerusalem."† And moreover—that the Lord will "have mercy on" the people of His scattered tribes, and fulfil to them His word, which said, "I will make all my mountains a way, and my highways shall be exalted. Behold these shall come from far; and lo!

* 2 Samuel xix. 16.   † Isaiah lxvi. 19, 20.

these from the land of Sinim (China)* . . . . .
The Children which thou shalt have after thou hast
lost the other, shall say again in thine ears, The
place is too straight for me: give place to me that I
may dwell.   Then shalt thou say in thine heart, Who
hath begotten me these, seeing I have lost my children and am desolate, a captive, and removing to
and fro?   And who hath brought up these?   Behold
I was left alone; *these, where had they been?*   Thus
saith the Lord God, Behold, I will lift up mine hand
to the Gentiles, and set my standard to the people;
and they shall bring thy sons in their arms, and thy
daughters shall be carried upon their shoulders; and
kings shall be thy nursing fathers (thy nourishers)
and their queens thy nursing mothers: they shall
bow down to thee with their face toward the earth.
. . . . I will contend with him that contendeth with
thee, and I will save thy children.†

So, when the Lord shall have descended, He shall
bow the heart of ALL THE REMNANT, to the interests
of Israel,—and they shall search them out in every
nation under heaven, and bring them to their own

---

* That the country which Isaiah called "Sinim" is the same as
that known to us as "China," is, at least, extremely probable. The
context plainly shows that it must be a country lying either east or
south of Israel. The word is very nearly allied to Sin, or Tcin, or
Tshini, by which name the people of China were known to the
Arabians and Syrians. GESENIUS says, "I understand it to be the
land of the Seres, or Chinese, Sinenses." CALMET refers to Mr.
Taylor, Dr. Morrison, and Dr. Hagar in proof that China is intended. KITTO says, "many Biblical Geographers think this may possibly denote the Sinese or Chinese, whose country is Sina, China.
This view is not void of probability."

† Isaiah xlix. 11—25.

land, that they may occupy it in an undisturbed possession, "from the wilderness and Lebanon, from the river, the river Euphrates, even unto the uttermost sea." (A vast territory, as we have seen in a former chapter, comprehending probably the whole, or nearly the whole peninsula of Arabia.*) And thus—"ALL Israel shall be saved; as it is written, There shall come out of Zion the Deliverer, that shall turn away ungodliness from Jacob, ... For the gifts and callings of God, are without repentance."†

ISRAEL thus restored in full, will be the people specially honored among all the nations of the earth, as those in whose midst the presence of the Lord will be made manifest during the Millennial age. In their Capital He will show forth His glory. In their restored JERUSALEM will be THE SANCTUARY in which He will delight, and unto which, as to the hallowed centre of the world, all nations shall approach with reverence and joy. THEIR RESTORATION WILL BE THE FIRST GREAT ACT OF THE MESSIAH, when, having overthrown the powers of evil, He will take His seat upon the Throne as "KING OVER ALL THE EARTH."‡

But before we speak particularly as to the *glorious manifestation* and *divine government* of the Messiah, let us give a passing consideration to the PHYSICAL, MORAL, and RELIGIOUS STATE of the earth, and of those people, who are to dwell upon it under the triumphant reign of the GREAT KING.

It is certainly wrong to suppose that the tremendous conflagration upon which ST. PETER dwells in

---

* See Chapter III., page 51.   † Romans xi. 26—29.
‡ Zechariah xiv. 9.

his *second epistle*, will take place at the *introduction*
of the *Reign of Peace.** It will occur, indeed, *in*
"the day of the Lord," but *not at its commencement.*
The Millennial age will *precede* it. We shall see
this clearly as we advance with our subjects. Yet
GREAT PHYSICAL CHANGES there undoubtedly *will be*
when the Lord establishes His dominion.

At His coming, when His feet shall stand upon
the Mount of Olives, ZECHARIAH tells us that the
mountain "shall cleave in the midst thereof towards
the east and towards the west, and there shall be a
very great valley: and half of the mountain shall
remove toward the north, and half of it toward the
south." And then addressing Israel, he says, "And
ye shall flee to the valley of the mountains, for the
valley of the mountains shall reach unto Azal; yea,
ye shall flee, like as ye fled from before the earthquake in the days of Uzziah, king of Judah."
Indeed there will be *good reasons* for a hasty flight;
for if (as is no doubt the case) AZAL be another name
for ASCALON, and a deep valley be formed, reaching
from ASCALON across the country and dividing the
Mount of Olives towards the DEAD SEA, we know
what must be the issue. The level of the Dead Sea
being *many hundreds of feet* below that of the Mediterranean, the waters of the latter sea will speedily
rush in. But to use the language of Major Phillips
in his interesting work "Interpretations of Prophecy,"—"The living waters of the ocean falling a
total of nearly eight times the fall of Niagara, with
an average descent of twenty-two feet per mile on

* 2 Peter iii. 10.

sixty miles, and entering the Dead Sea at the Northern Extremity, will speedily cause its waters to rise; and while a mighty whirlpool will be created in the vast basin of the Dead Sea, the rising waters will be quietly permeating the drift sands of four thousand years, which now conceal the southern bed of the river Jordan. Yes, as surely as the waters of the Mediterranean will enter the Dead Sea at an angle, and admirably prepared as the geographical construction of its surrounding mountains is, to produce a grand gyration, so surely will that gyration of commingled waters rise from a hollow swirl, to a mighty overpowering swell. And when at length the waters stand upon an heap, (as Scripture phrases it), and the sustaining power of gyration ceases to uphold, the mass of water falls, and separates, and strikes against the surrounding mountain sides. And now, 'Let the sea roar, and the fulness thereof; let the floods clap their hands before the Lord, for He cometh to judge the earth, and the people with His righteousness; and God will make a way in the wilderness and rivers in the desert.' The tumultuous waters finding no other outlet, will rush down the Jordan's bed, cleansing it as in a moment. The Dead Sea, rising above its desolated shores, will overflow by the valley of Edom, completing the straits of AZAL into the long Red Sea, by the Gulf of Akabah. Thus, JERUSALEM, BECOMING THE CENTRAL CITY OF THE EARTH, WILL STAND UPON THE HIGHWAY FOR ALL NATIONS."

So, can we understand how there will be a fulfilment of divers prophecies, which are otherwise enveloped in deep mystery. That, for example, in the *ninety-seventh* PSALM, which indeed gives us the outline of the whole course of events immediately consequent upon the Advent.—"THE LORD REIGNETH, let the earth rejoice; let the multitude of isles be glad thereof. Clouds and darkness are round about Him: righteousness and judgment are the habitation of His throne. A fire goeth before Him, and burneth up His enemies round about. His lightnings enlightened the world: the earth saw and trembled. THE HILLS MELTED LIKE WAX AT THE PRESENCE OF THE LORD, AT THE PRESENCE OF THE LORD OF THE WHOLE EARTH. The heavens declare His righteousness, and all people have seen His glory." Or again —in the Prophet MICAH, the *first chapter*—"Behold, the Lord cometh forth out of His place, and will *come down, and tread upon the high places of the earth.* AND THE MOUNTAINS SHALL BE MOLTEN UNDER HIM, AND THE VALLEYS SHALL BE CLEFT, AS WAX BEFORE THE FIRE, AND AS THE WATERS THAT ARE POURED DOWN A STEEP PLACE." Or again; in HOSEA, the *second chapter*, speaking of "that day" wherein "saith the Lord .... thou shalt call me Ishi (my husband) and shalt call me no more Baali (my lord)," it is added,—"Behold I will allure her, and bring her *into the wilderness,* and speak comfortably unto her. And I will give her vineyards *from thence,* and THE VALLEY OF ACHOR (a valley in the neighborhood of Gilgal and Jericho) FOR A DOOR OF HOPE; and she shall sing there, as in the days of her youth, and as in the day when she came up out of the land of Egypt."

Or once again;—in JOEL, the *third chapter*,—"And it shall come to pass in that day, that the mountains shall drop down new wine, and the hills shall flow with milk, and all the rivers of Judah shall flow with waters, and *a fountain shall come forth of the house of the Lord, and shall water* THE VALLEY OF SHITTIM." (Shittim lies E.N.E. of Jerusalem, by the river Jordan.*)

And thus, Jerusalem will become a city, fit, by reason of its situation, to be esteemed the capital of the whole world. Close at hand will be the Dead Sea,—*but with its waters healed*, so that, as EZEKIEL tells us, "the *fishers* shall stand upon it from Engedi even unto Eneglaim;"† and the lake converted into a vast pool of shelter for *shipping*, will be entered on the north by the straits flowing from the Mediterranean, and on the south by those which will unite its waters with the Red Sea. With such a change effected, who could select a spot so favorable as JERUSALEM for the situation of THE EARTH'S METROPOLIS.

But let us note the whole passage of EZEKIEL'S prophecy from which we have just quoted a sentence. In the *first verse* of the *forty-seventh chapter* the Prophet begins to relate a point of his remarkable vision of the days of the Messiah's kingdom, and says—"He brought me again unto the door of the house (the new Temple); and behold, waters issued out from under the threshold of the house *eastward*: for the forefront of the house stood toward the east, and the waters came down from under, from the right

---

* Num ers xxxiii. 49, 50.　　† Ezekiel xlvii. 10.

side of the house, at the south side of the altar.* Then brought he me out of the way of the gate northward, and led me about the way without unto the outer gate by the way that looketh eastward; and behold *there ran out water on the right side.* (That is to say, perhaps, the waters issuing "from under the threshold of the Temple," flowed rather to the south of the east.) And when the man that had the line in his hand went forth eastward, he measured a thousand cubits, and he brought me through the waters; and the waters were to the ankles. Again he measured a thousand cubits, and brought me through the waters; the waters were to the knees. Again he measured a thousand, and brought me

---

* A well-known engineer, named Pierotti, has discovered that the present city of Jerusalem is built on several layers of masonry, each layer pertaining to a different age. He is of opinion that the lowest layer, which is composed of very large stone-, is of the time of Solomon; the next above it, of the days of Zerubbabel; the third, of the reign of King Herod; the fourth of the time of Justinian, and so on. He has found a series of water conduits leading *from the place where the Temple stood* to the valley of Jehoshaphat. He has discovered, moreover, a fountain at the pool of Bethesda, from which, upon its being open, a considerable stream of water began to flow, and has flowed ever since. No one can tell its source, nor can they discover the place which finally receives its flood.

A letter from Jerusalem, dated March 17th, 1862, says, "I had a good opportunity of seeing the temple enclosure. *Wishing to see the water for myself,* I went down. By the side of El-Aksa is the entrance to the subterranean water. You descend a few steps, and then jump into a hole. Before you is a door cut out of the rock; you still see he places for the Kings. You pass this doorway, and descend a flight of broad steps to the edge of the water, which is delightful, very cold, about four feet deep, and pebbly at the bottom, as if it were spring water. It is not known how far it extends. It branches off in every direction; and in the water are large irregular pillars." *Quarterly Journal of Prophecy,* October, 1862.

through; the waters were to the loins. Afterwards he *l* measured a thousand; and it was a river that I could not pass over.* .... Then said he unto me, These waters issue out *towards the east country*, (that is in the direction of the northern point of the Dead Sea) and down into the Desert (or plain), and go into the Sea (the Dead Sea); which (waters) being brought forth into the Sea, the waters (of the Sea) *shall be healed*. And it shall come to pass that everything that liveth, which moveth whithersoever the rivers shall come, shall live: and there shall be a very great multitude of fish, because these waters shall come thither: for they shall be healed; and everything shall live whither the river cometh. And it shall come to pass, that the fishers shall stand upon it from Engedi even to Eneglaim: they shall be a place to spread forth nets; their fish shall be according to their kinds AS THE FISH OF THE GREAT SEA (the Mediterreanean), exceeding many." Surely no one can consider this to be mere *figurative* language. It speaks for itself, that *there shall be material physical changes in the neighborhood of Jerusalem;* changes which shall place the city in a position *far* more favorable than that which it at present occupies.

Nor are these all the changes which are to affect the neighborhood of Zion when the Lord shall come. For we read in the *fourteenth chapter* of ZECHARIAH that—"All the land shall be turned as a plain, from

---

* This will, no doubt, be a stream of spring water, flowing in a S.E. direction from the temple, until it meets the Straits which are to cross the country from the Mediterranean to the north of the Dead Sea.

GEBA to RIMMON, south of Jerusalem, and it shall be lifted up." Now GEBA was a city of Benjamin, a few miles north of Jerusalem;* and RIMMON was a city of Judah on the southern boundary.† Thus *a vast extent of table land* will be formed, for an important purpose, which will be brought forward presently. For the moment, let it suffice to mention it, and pass on to observe changes which will take place elsewhere. We read that desert places are to teem with vegetable life and beauty. For example: Idumea is spoken of; and after its judgments are proclaimed, it is added— "The desert shall rejoice and blossom as the rose. It shall blossom abundantly, and rejoice even with joy and singing; the glory of Lebanon shall be given unto it, the excellency of Carmel and Sharon . . . . the parched ground shall become a pool, and the thirsty land springs of water . . . . and an highway shall be there;" and this shall be when "the ransomed of the Lord shall return and come to Zion with songs and everlasting joy upon their heads."‡ And so again, (but not, it would appear, of any one place particularly),—"Behold, I will do a new thing; now it shall spring forth; shall ye not know it? I will even make a way in the wilderness, and rivers in the desert. The beasts of the field shall honor me, the dragons and the owls: because I give waters in the wilderness and rivers in the desert, to give drink to my people, my chosen."

True, it *may* be only the land of Israel (as it shall then be) which will become the subject of these

---

* Joshua xxviii. 24, and xxi. 17.   † Joshua xv. 21—32.
‡ Isaiah xxxiv. and xxxv.

changes, but there *is reason* to believe that they will be *general*, for the *whole world* is evidently called to the rejoicings of the millennial period; and the Lord is not to be King over Israel only,—but OVER ALL THE EARTH." *It must be enough for us, however, that we accept the limits of the Scripture word.* For the rest, the Lord will show us in His own good time.

But now that we are speaking of the physical changes, which will affect man's comfort,—we must not overlook what is said so plainly about a *wondrous transformation* of which those LOWER ANIMALS, which now prey upon each other, and are wont to make attack upon the life of men, will be the subjects. How it *can be* I will not stay to ask—"with God ALL THINGS are possible." That it *will be*, is distinctly stated; and it is enough. These ravenous beasts *shall never more destroy* when the Redeemer's reign of peace shall be established; for the mouth of the Lord hath spoken it. He who could first *form*, can, when He pleases *re-form:* and RE-FORM HE WILL. "Behold, I create new heavens, and a new earth: and the former shall not be remembered nor come into mind. . . . . The wolf and the lamb shall feed together, and the lion shall eat straw like the bullock; and dust shall be the serpent's meat. They shall not hurt nor destroy in all my holy mountain, saith the Lord."*

BUT WHEN SHALL ALL THIS BE? the same prophet—ISAIAH, by whom these last words were spoken, tells us in the *eleventh chapter* that it shall be *when* the "Rod out of the stem of Jesse," and the "Branch

* Isaiah lxv. 17—25.

out of his roots" shall come forth; that King who
shall "with righteousness .... judge the poor, and
reprove with equity for the meek of the earth," the
girdle of whose loins, moreover, shall be "righteousness," and "faithfulness the girdle of His reins.
And further, that it shall be *when* the Lord shall set
His hand *again the second time* to recover the remnant of His people which shall be left .... the outcasts of Israel and the dispersed of Judah;" *when*
"the envy also of Ephraim shall depart, and the
adversaries of Judah shall be cut off," and "Ephraim
shall not envy Judah," and "Judah shall not vex
Ephraim;" and *when* the word shall sound forth from
the length and breadth of earth, "cry out and shout,
thou inhabitant of Zion; for great is the Holy One
of Israel in the midst of thee." THEN shall be
THAT HAPPY DAY OF PEACE among the wonders of
which it is declared repeatedly "The wolf also shall
dwell with the lamb, and the leopard shall lie down
with the kid; and the calf, and the young lion, and
the fatling together; and a little child shall lead
them. And the cow and the bear shall feed; their
young ones shall lie down together; and the lion
shall eat straw like the ox. And the sucking child
shall play on the hole of the asp, and the weaned
child shall put his hand on the cockatrice's den.
They shall not hurt nor destroy in all my holy
mountain; for the earth shall be full of the knowledge
of the Lord, as the waters cover the sea.* Surely it
cannot be WISDOM's part to *cavil at* or *explain away*,
or try to *spiritualize* such passages as these. It is

* Isaiah xi. and lxv.

better to *receive with meekness* what the Lord has spoken, and *submissively adore.* *Our* IMPOSSIBILITIES are *God's* SIMPLICITIES. How foolish many a *learned reasoner* of earth will look, when in the presence of his *untutored neighbor*, in the day of Christ! The *garb of his philosophy;* his *wise conclusions;* his *"cannot be"* and *"must be"* all departed; and his soul, through earthly wisdom, standing wrapped in folly; while that soul of simple, childlike faith, which had been wont on earth to lay its hand upon its mouth, and meekly listen to the word of God; and, *not having seen or even understood*, yet had believed, and prayed for a sufficient light, and rendered thanks to God for every little gleam from heaven,—*shall stand forth adorned in wisdom, such as the All-Wise will look upon with approbation.*

But let us turn now from the *lower creatures*, and consider MAN'S ESTATE during the Lord's reign of Peace.

We must not fall into the error of confounding the *millennial* state with that of *final glory.* In the former state, the earth will be inhabited just as it has been throughout previous ages; children will be born, and those who have fulfilled their years will die. There will be *peace,* but *not perfection:*—Comparative, but *not perfect* righteousness. The change will be great, but not a change like that from earth to *heaven.* It will be *earth still*, and man *in fallen nature* will be earth's inhabitant. Yet man will undergo a change: his state will not be just what it is now. But we will see what God has taught concerning this. We will refer to the *sixty-fifth chapter* of ISAIAH, in which that day is spoken of, wherein "the wolf and the lamb shall feed together, ... and they shall not hurt nor destroy." Here we find also the grand promise which God made to Israel—"I will rejoice in Jerusalem, and joy in my people: and the voice of weeping shall be no more heard in her, nor the voice of crying. There shall be no more thence an infant of days, nor an old man that hath not filled his days; *for the child shall die an hundred years old.* . . . . And they shall build houses and inhabit them, and they shall plant vineyards and eat the fruit of them. They shall not build, and *another* inhabit; they shall not plant, and *another* eat: for *as the days of a tree* are the days of my people; and *mine elect shall long enjoy the work of their own hands.*" .

So it is evident that *there will be death*, ("the child shall *die.*") But it is evident also that the life of man will be *prolonged*, perhaps as in the days of the early Patriarchs, (as the days *of a tree*, are the days of my people;) so that the constitution of man will have received a new supply of strength. As he passes on through life, however, there will be warning voices telling him that this is not his home. He will not wholly escape sickness: wherefore *trees* are spoken of as abounding by the waters of the regenerated Israel, of which the fruit "shall be for meat, *and the leaf thereof for* MEDICINE."*

But let us now glance upon what is said respecting THINGS SPIRITUAL in the Reign of Peace.

And first, concerning MAN: as we have just now

* Ezekiel xlvii. 12.

seen, he will be still the subject of affliction, sickness, and death. This would *not* be, surely, if he were *sinless;* for *death is* emphatically declared to be THE WAGES OF SIN.* Indeed the Prophet ISAIAH, in the chapter from which we have just now been quoting, very plainly intimates that *there shall be sin,*—saying—"*The sinner* being an hundred years old, shall be *accursed.*" ZECHARIAH too, leads us to the same conclusion in the latter part of the *fourteenth chapter,* where he says—"And it shall come to pass, that every one that is left of all the nations which came against Jerusalem, shall even go up from year to year to worship the King, the Lord of Hosts, and to keep the Feast of Tabernacles. And it shall be, that *whoso will not come up of all the families of the earth unto Jerusalem to worship the King, the 'Lord of Hosts, even upon them shall be no rain.* And if the family of Egypt go not up, and come not, that have no rain, there shall be the plague wherewith the Lord will smite the heathen that come not up to keep the Feast of Tabernacles. *This shall be the punishment of Egypt, and the punishment of all nations that come not up to keep the Feast of Tabernacles.*" So, doubtless, as there will be *death,* there will be SIN, and CURSE because of sin. Yet sin will not be *rampant.* Open transgression will, no doubt, be *rare:* for although mankind will still retain the flesh, just as of old,—*unregenerated, unaltered, as prone as ever to iniquity,*—so that therein will dwell "no good thing," and the unholy law thereof will be as truly adverse to "the law" of the regenerated mind,

* Romans vi. 23.

as it is *now*, or as it was when the Apostle wrote concerning it;* yet the *prompting power* will be removed; Satan will be bound; and all temptation from the spiritual powers of evil will have ceased. Moreover, there will be *no room* for unbelief or doubt: for "the knowledge of the glory of the Lord shall cover the earth, as the waters cover the seas."† And besides this, the righteous government of the Almighty King will favor righteous dealing among all people. The evidence of perfect love controlling all things with regard to man, will favor kindly feeling, charitable action, and an open, generous demeanor.

Thus, although the earth, beneath the sway of the long promised sceptre, *will not be transformed into heaven*, yet it will be greatly changed, and become, as it were, "a *new* earth," in which righteousness, and peace, and confidence, and love, will everywhere abound; and wherein those who will not give their hearts to God, will be but few and hidden.

But now let us look *higher;* and consider for awhile THE KING OF KINGS and his associates in government. "Behold a King shall reign in righteousness, and Princes shall execute judgment."‡—Behold the days come, saith the Lord, that I will raise unto David a Righteous Branch, and a King shall reign and prosper, and shall execute judgment and justice in the earth. In his days Judah shall be saved, and Israel shall dwell safely: and this is His name, whereby He shall be called, THE LORD OUR RIGHT-

---

* Romans vii. 14—25.   † Isaiah xi. 9. Habakkuk ii. 14.
‡ Isaiah xxxii. 1.

EOUSNESS.*—The Lord "shall reign in Mount Zion, and in Jerusalem, and among his ancients, gloriously."†—The Lord "shall be king over all the earth."‡—The Lord shall receive the heathen for his inheritance, and the uttermost parts of the earth for his possession; and, having broken the wicked as with a rod of iron, dashed them in pieces like a potter's vessel,§ and destroyed them with the sword of His justice; He shall reign in undisturbed possession, "KING OF KINGS, and LORD OF LORDS;" and His name shall be called, WONDERFUL, COUNSELLOR, THE MIGHTY GOD, THE EVERLASTING FATHER, THE PRINCE OF PEACE."‖ HE SHALL REIGN.—Of this there is no room for doubt.

But, now in speaking of His Reign, we must confess a difficulty.

We have seen, I believe, clearly, that the Lord will descend from Heaven *in his manhood;* and that *as Son of Man* He will "stand upon the Mount of Olives," and sit upon the throne of His glory." Indeed, it must be clear to every candid reader of the prophecies, that the Lord will, *in His human nature* rendered glorious in the glory of the father, stand upon the earth, and as the King, *whose right it is,* ascend the throne of David, both to order and establish the kingdom of that honored prince, with judgment and with justice. The testimony is of the fullest and the plainest kind, and cannot be gainsayed.

But are we *obliged* therefore, to understand that

---

* Jeremiah xxii. 5, 6   † Isaiah xxiv. 23.   ‡ Zechariah xiv. 9.
§ Psalm ii.   ‖ Isaiah ix. 6.

the Lord Jesus Christ will really make this earth
again His *dwelling-place?* that He will actually, and
for the period of a thousand years *make this world
His abode?* He *may* indeed. But I do not think
the evidence is strong enough for us to say "HE
WILL." It appears indeed to my mind very certain
that HE WILL NOT make earth the *residence* of His
glorified body: but that He will—for the period of
the Millennial age—inhabit *the Jerusalem above,*—the
"NEW JERUSALEM" which is to come out of Heaven
from God,* of which the glory of God and of the
Lamb is the light. Of this "New Jerusalem" we
shall have to speak particularly in another chapter.
Let it suffice now, that it will probably be *within
sight of the inhabitants of earth,* and will be known
as the glorious abode of Christ, and the vast company
of His risen saints; so that there will be *a constant
evidence* afforded of the *reality of the* Redeemer's
reign, and of the *bliss of his redeemed people.* The
residence of the Great King in this abode of glory,
need not prevent His acting towards mankind *as He
was wont to act in days of early innocence,* when He
came down and visited the Garden of Eden, and
there conversed with our *first parents* as their constant FRIEND and COUNSELLOR. And why may He
not condescend to such an intercourse again? Why
may He not descend from time to time, and visit the
Millennial earth, that men may be inspired with
higher confidence and purer love? The tone of the
prophetic word most certainly shows favor to the
opinion that He *will* do so. But if so, then we need

* Revelation xxi.

not pause to question *how* or *where* a *fitting residence* shall be prepared by God for His abode upon the hallowed height (a matter full of serious difficulties); but we can hold the doctrine of His reign as King over the whole earth, and in a special manner as the KING OF ISRAEL,

But we have material aid in support of this view from the two Prophets, JEREMIAH and EZEKIEL.

To prepare ourselves for their remarkable assertions, we will call to mind the testimony afforded us in Scripture to the fact that the GLORIFIED SAINTS *shall occupy important places in the government of Israel and of the world.* OUR SAVIOUR told His apostles that it should be so." "In the regeneration" said He "when the SON OF MAN shall sit on the throne of His glory, YE ALSO SHALL SIT ON TWELVE THRONES JUDGING THE TWELVE TRIBES OF ISRAEL.* St. PAUL, rebuking the Corinthians for divisions, which they suffered to exist, demanded of them,— "Do ye not know that THE SAINTS SHALL JUDGE THE WORLD.† So too, ST. JOHN in the *twentieth chapter* of the REVELATION, tells us,—"And I saw THRONES AND THEY SAT UPON THEM, AND JUDGMENT WAS GIVEN UNTO THEM; and I saw the souls of them that were beheaded for the witness of Jesus, and for the word of God, and which had not worshipped the beast neither his image; neither had received his mark upon their foreheads, or in their hands; AND THEY LIVED AND REIGNED WITH CHRIST A THOUSAND YEARS." It is quite certain, then, that judgment shall, in some sense and degree, *"be delivered unto*

* Matthew xix. 28.   † 1 Cor. vi. 2.

the Saints," and that, as DANIEL tells us,—"The kingdom and dominion, and the greatness of the kingdom under the whole heaven shall be given *to the people of the Saints of the Most High,* whose kingdom is an everlasting kingdom, and all dominions shall serve and obey Him."*

In speaking of the share which shall be granted to the saints of Jesus in the Millennial kingdom, we must not omit to notice a point of very interesting, and—to Israel especially—of heart-stirring, kind. I mean, THE VICE-ROYALTY OF THE RISEN DAVID. This is the subject to which I referred as aiding the doctrine that the Lord shall indeed reign over the earth, but having His abode in "the New Jerusalem" above.

If we turn to JEREMIAH, the *thirtieth chapter,* we find the Prophet descanting in language which we have already quoted, upon Jacob's trouble and deliverance. In the *eighth verse* we read thus—"It shall come to pass in that day, saith the Lord of Hosts, that I will break *his* yoke† from off thy neck, and will burst thy bonds, and strangers shall no more serve themselves of him: but they shall serve THE LORD their GOD, and DAVID THEIR KING, WHOM I WILL RAISE UP UNTO THEM. Therefore, fear thou not, O my servant Jacob, saith the Lord."

Now if this passage stood alone, we should be tempted, perhaps, to pass it over without any great

---

* Daniel vii. 27.

† The yoke of *some one* who shall have dominion in "the day of Jacob's trouble." The context plainly shows that he is "the Antichrist." Read chapters xxx. and xxxi.

regard; for, its subject is *extraordinary*, and the idea would be readily encouraged that some *hidden* interpretation must be correct, instead of that which is at once apparent. We should be tempted to consider, perhaps, that the name of DAVID was given to CHRIST, he being David's "Root and Offspring;" and that A SPIRITUAL, or PERSONAL, REIGN OF THE MESSIAH was intended to be understood. But the passage we have quoted is supported *far too strongly* to allow of this. *It is evidently to be taken as it stands.* But let us refer *elsewhere* respecting it. In the *thirty-fourth chapter* of EZEKIEL we find much said about the Restoration of the Tribes of Israel, when the Lord "will gather them from the countries, and will bring them to their own land, and feed them upon the mountains of Israel." Many, and replete with consolation, are the words which are spoken about those who shall be brought from the dispersion. The Lord speaks of them as His sheep, and of Himself as their careful owner; and says, "I will save my flock, and they shall be no more a prey; and I will judge between cattle and cattle. And I will set up ONE SHEPHERD over them, and he shall feed them, even MY SERVANT DAVID: He shall feed them, and He shall be their shepherd. And I THE LORD will be THEIR GOD, and MY SERVANT DAVID A PRINCE AMONG THEM. I the Lord have spoken it." Now, certainly, in this place it is *not possible* for "DAVID" to be put for "THE LORD," because the Lord speaks of Himself *separately*. "I THE LORD will be THEIR GOD, and MY SERVANT DAVID a PRINCE AMONG THEM."

But further; in Ezekiel, the *thirty-seventh chapter*, where the subject of Israel's restoration is again introduced, and God declares,—"I will make them (Israel and Judah) ONE NATION, in the land, upon the mountains of Israel; and ONE KING shall be KING TO THEM ALL: and they shall be no more two nations, neither shall they be divided into two kingdoms any more at all: neither shall they defile themselves any more with idols, nor with their detestable things, nor with any of their transgressions . . . . SO THEY SHALL BE MY PEOPLE, AND I WILL BE THEIR GOD,"— He adds—"And DAVID MY SERVANT SHALL BE KING OVER THEM, and they shall all have ONE SHEPHERD: they shall also walk in my judgments, and observe my statutes and do them. And they shall dwell in the land that I have given unto Jacob my servant, wherein your fathers have dwelt: and they shall dwell therein, even they and their children, and their children's children, for ever; and MY SERVANT DAVID SHALL BE THEIR PRINCE FOR EVER . . . my tabernacle also shall be with them; yea, I WILL BE THEIR GOD, and they shall be my people.

Now, I do not think that any language can speak plainer than this. *Why should we assume that it is figurative?* Would we presume to say "*It cannot be*" when God has thus repeatedly and unequivocally declared "IT SHALL BE." Nay, rather, let us here, as elsewhere, take God's word as simple truth, whether it agree or disagree with any preconceived ideas of ours. Indeed, what *friend of Israel* would desire to explain such a declaration otherwise than as it stands? For what should be a greater joy to the

Twelve Tribes, when in possession of their Covenant-inheritance, than to find their ancient, well-beloved DAVID also given them TO BE THEIR KING? O who is he who would not praise the Lord for such amazing proof of love towards Israel!

We may conclude, then, that KING DAVID AND THE OTHER SAINTS OF CHRIST shall occupy appointed places in the government and judgment of this world. Like Christ, it is quite possible they may not *live on earth;* they may perhaps only *visit* it from time to time. No information has been given as to this; nor is it needful we should know particulars concerning it, until the day of Christ arrives. Let it suffice that *fact it is,*—THE LORD SHALL REIGN SUPREME, the KING OF KINGS. DAVID, as the chief Vice-Roi of Christ, shall be the KING OF ISRAEL. The other SAINTS shall REIGN WITH CHRIST, and JUDGE THE WORLD. So then, as the Prophet bids us, let us "Behold, a King shall reign in righteousness, and Princes shall rule in judgment. And a man shall be as an hiding-place from the wind, and a covert from the tempest; as rivers of water in a dry place; as the shadow of a great rock in a weary land. And the eyes of them that see shall not be dim: and the ears of them that hear shall hearken. The heart also of the rash shall understand knowledge, and the tongue of the stammerers shall be ready to speak plainly."*

But now we have to speak of the RELIGIOUS WORSHIP which shall characterize the Reign of Peace. I do not see how it is possible to read the word of

* Isaiah xxxii. 1—4.

11

Prophecy concerning the Millennial Age, without arriving at the conclusion that A TEMPLE WILL BE ERECTED AT JERUSALEM, in which, during that happy period, the Lord shall manifest his glory, and declare His presence with His people.

Concerning this Temple, its glory and its service, much is told us in the Scriptures which we must proceed to note with care.

We have already spoken of the Temple which Israel will erect after their partial restoration under Antichrist. *This temple will undoubtedly be destroyed* at the coming of the Lord;—for not only will a great earthquake then divide the Mount of Olives, and form a chasm from Ascalon to the valley of Achor, but also "all the land shall be turned *as a plain*, from GEBA to RIMMON, south of Jerusalem: And it shall *be lifted up.*"* Doubtless, therefore, utter destruction will be the lot of every edifice erected in the neighborhood.

But, independently of this, it is quite evident that the Temple which the Jews will erect, or set about erecting, on their first restoration, will not be the Temple which is to adorn the Jerusalem of the Millennial age. At least, it is *exceedingly* improbable that it will be so, by reason of the *vast dimensions* given for the Millennial Temple and City, and the *brief period, consisting of seven years only*, which is to be allotted to the Jews, from their return under Antichrist to the dawn of "the Great Day." Indeed how much more reasonable is the supposition, that when the Lord shall come and establish His dominion

* Zechariah xiv. 4—10. See also pages 139, 140 of this chapter.

over the whole earth, if a Temple be required in the
renewed Jerusalem, it should be erected *then*. Nay,
it is declared that so *it shall be;* for if we turn to
ZECHARIAH, the *sixth chapter*, we find both the
HOUSE and its BUILDER, spoken of as follows:—
"Behold the man, whose name is THE BRANCH:
and He shall grow up out of His place, and HE SHALL
BUILD THE TEMPLE OF THE LORD: EVEN HE SHALL
BUILD THE TEMPLE OF THE LORD; and He shall bear
the glory, and He shall sit and rule upon His throne;
and He shall be a Priest upon His throne . . .
And they that are far off shall come and build in the
Temple of the Lord."

No doubt, then, we are to understand that when
the Lord has come, and has established His kingdom,
and manifested forth his glory in the sight of all men,
HE WILL DIRECT THE BUILDING OF A TEMPLE AS THE
GRAND CENTRE OF HIS WORSHIP, AND THE PLACE
WHERE HE MAY CHIEFLY HOLD COMMUNION WITH THE
SONS OF MEN. The wondrously exalted plain from
Geba to Rimmon, forming a site "beautiful for situation" upon which a city of great magnitude may be
built, the chief attraction in which will be the Temple
of the Lord, and the Shekinah of His presence. And
thus Jerusalem, "the city of the great King," will be
"THE JOY OF THE WHOLE EARTH."

The Lord had shown His servant EZEKIEL the
whole outline of events connected with the restoration
of Israel, the re-union of the twelve tribes, the reign
of the risen David, and other matters in which God's
people, in the "last day," will have intimate concern.
And now, as the remarkable prophecy draws towards

its close, the Lord would give His servant most minute instructions, with regard both to the City and the Temple of which we have been speaking.

In the *fourth chapter*, the Prophet is brought before us standing in the land of Israel "upon a very high mountain, by which was AS THE FRAME OF A CITY, towards the south." A man stood by the Prophet "with a line of flax in his hand, and a measuring reed." And he commenced a measurement of the Temple, which was in the city. The length of the reed with which he measured was *six cubits* and *six hand-breadths*. Therefore, about *ten feet six inches*, (taking the *cubit* at *eighteen inches* and the *hand-breadth* at *three inches*). The man began by the measurement of a wall which was round about the House, on which were erected many small chambers; and pursued his work, measuring the courts, the gateways, the porches, and at length the main building of the Temple itself. Now the extreme length of each side of the surrounding wall, was *five hundred reeds*, or about five thousand two hundred and fifty *feet*, that is to say A MILE all but thirty feet. This would make the Temple and its enclosure about equal to the greatest extent reached by the entire ancient city of Jerusalem, the circumference of which (according to Josephus) was *thirty-three stadia*, or *three and a half geographical miles*, nearly.*

---

* The measurement of the Millennial *Jerusalem* is given in the 48th chapter of Ezekiel. The length of each of the four sides is four thousand five hundred measures (*i. e.* measuring-reeds of 10¼ feet): equal therefore to forty-seven thousand two hundred and fifty feet, or nearly NINE MILES. To that the whole circumference of the city is to be about THIRTY-SIX MILES.

I must refer my readers to their Bibles for the whole details of the wondrous Temple. The Prophet has minutely given them, and his language is so plain that no interpreter is needed.

To one point, however, I would direct attention, since it has been a matter of interesting inquiry to many students of the prophecies. Will there be, or will there not be, A RESTITUTION OF THE MOSAIC SACRIFICES, in the millennial Temple? Sacrifices, *commemorative* of what Christ HAS DONE, instead of, (as they were of old,) *the types* of what Christ WAS TO DO?

Concerning this, as every other subject, the plain assertions of the Word of God must be CONCLUSIVE. We are not to refuse our credence to the thing revealed, because *we cannot see* how it will harmonize with other matters in the Lord's economy. The spirit which the zealous Peter manifested when he said—"Be it far from Thee Lord, this shall not be unto Thee," was not good. The Lord rebuked it,— saying, "Get thee behind me Satan, thou art an offence unto me; for thou savourest not the things that be of God, but those that be of men."*

Resolved then to take the word of God *as we find it*, we will follow the course of those chapters—the *fortieth* to the *forty-sixth* inclusive—which describe the Temple; noting those passages which have im- mediately reference to this matter. Taking first, then, the *fortieth* chapter, we pass over the minute particu- lars as to chambers, gates, windows, and ornaments, until we reach the *thirty-eight verse*, from which place

* Matthew xvi. 22, 23.

and onward we read as follows:—"And the chambers, and the entries thereof, were by the posts of the gates, *where they washed the burnt-offering.* And in the porch of the gate were two tables on this side, and two tables on that side, *to slay thereon the burnt-offering, and the sin-offering, and the trespass-offering. . . . .* Four tables were on this side, and four tables on that side, by the side of the gate; eight tables, *whereupon they slew their sacrifices;* and the four tables were of hewn stone for *the burnt-offering,* of a cubit and a half long, and a cubit and a half broad and one cubit high; *whereupon also they laid the instruments where-with they slew the burnt-offering and the sacrifice.* And within were hooks an hand broad, fastened round about; and *upon the tables was the flesh of the offering."* But again let us pass on, until we come to the *thirteenth verse* of the *forty-second chapter,* where it is declared of certain chambers, that therein "the Priests that approach unto the LORD, shall eat the most holy things; there they shall lay the most holy things, and *the meat-offering, and the sin-offering, and the trespass-offering."* Then passing on to the *next chapter,* at the *thirteenth verse* we find minute instructions given about the ALTAR and the SACRIFICES, which are more conclusive still. "And these are the measures of the altar after the cubits (the cubit is a cubit of an hand-breadth). . . . . The altar shall be four cubits; and from the altar and upwards shall be four horns. And the altar shall be twelve cubits long, twelve broad, square in the four squares thereof. . . . . And he said unto me, Son of man, *thus saith the Lord God,* These are the ordinances of the altar, in the day when they shall make it, *to offer burnt-offerings thereon and to sprinkle blood thereon.* And thou shalt give to the priests, the Levites that be of the seed of Zadok, which approach unto me, to minister unto me, saith the Lord God, *a young bullock for a sin-offering.* And *thou shalt take of the blood thereof,* and put it on the four horns of it, and on the four corners of the settle, and upon the border round about; thus shalt thou cleanse and purge it. Thou shalt take *the bullock also of the sin-offering,* and he shall burn it in the appointed place of the house, without the sanctuary. And on the second day *thou shalt offer a kid of the goats without blemish for a sin-offering;* and they shall cleanse the altar, as they did cleanse it with the bullock. And when thou hast made an end of cleansing it, *thou shalt offer a young bullock without blemish, and a ram out of the flock without blemish.* And thou shalt offer them before the Lord. . . . . Seven days shalt thou prepare every day a goat for a sin-offering: they shall also prepare a young bullock, and a ram out of the flock, without blemish . . . . and when these days are expired, it shall be that upon the eighth day, and so forward, *the priests shall make your burnt-offerings upon the altar, and your peace-offerings;* AND I WILL ACCEPT YOU, SAITH THE LORD GOD." But further, let us note the language of the *forty-fifth chapter.* Here again we have the particular sacrifices which are to be offered, brought before us,—and "THE PRINCE"* is spoken of

---

* No doubt "the Prince" is David, as we have seen in commenting on the 37th chapter: where we read—"My servant David shall be *their prince* for ever."

as having an important office to fulfil in connection with the offerings. If we refer to the *fifteenth verse* we read thus,—"*One lamb out of the flock, out of two hundred, out of the fat pastures of Israel, for a meat-offering, and for a burnt-offering, and for peace-offerings, to make reconciliation for them, saith the Lord God.* All the people of the land shall give this oblation *for the prince* in Israel. And it shall be *the prince's part to give burnt-offerings, and meat-offerings, and drink-offerings,* in the feasts, and in the new-moons, and in the Sabbaths, in all solemnities of the house of Israel: *he shall prepare the sin-offering, and the meat-offering, and the burnt-offering, and the peace-offering, to make reconciliation for the house of Israel.*" But we need not quote further, though there remains much wherewith to strengthen our position, and give force to our assertion—THAT GOD HAS TOLD US PLAINLY THAT THERE SHALL BE SACRIFICES ACTUALLY OFFERED UPON THE ALTAR OF THE LORD IN THAT TEMPLE WHICH IS TO BE THE GLORY OF THE MILLENNIAL JERUSALEM:—SACRIFICES, COMMEMORATIVE OF THE SEVERAL POINTS AND BEARINGS OF THE FINISHED WORK OF THE LORD JESUS CHRIST. If EZEKIEL's language in this case be *figurative*, I know not where in the whole word of God we can find any, as to which we have a right to say that *it is literal.*

But we must refer to *other* prophecies, before we close the subject of this Temple and its services; and see if they give any information which will throw light upon it.

ISAIAH plainly speaks of the Millennial TEMPLE,

in the *second chapter*, as an exalted place into which "all nations shall flow," and from which the law and the word of the Lord shall go forth. In the *sixty-sixth chapter* also, we find God speaking of the *Priests* and *Levites* whom He will appoint in the day of Israel's restoration, when the tribes shall be brought out of all nations as an offering unto the Lord.

JEREMIAH tells us in the *thirteenth chapter*, "Thus saith the LORD, Behold, I will bring again the captivity of Jacob's tents, and have mercy on his dwelling places; *and the city shall be builded* upon her own heap, and THE PALACE shall remain after the fashion therof. And out of them shall proceed thanksgiving. .... In the latter days ye shall consider it." Again in the *thirty-third chapter.*—"*Neither shall the priests, the Levites, want a man before me to offer burnt-offerings, and to kindle meat-offerings, and to do sacrifice continually.*"

MICAH does not allow the Temple of the last days to pass unnoticed. He speaks of it in the *fourth chapter* of his prophecy, almost in the same words as those which were used by Isaiah—"In the last days it shall come to pass that the mountain of *the house of the Lord* shall be established in the top of the mountains .... and many nations shall come, and say, come, and let us go up to the mountain of the Lord, and *to the House of the God of Jacob*, and He will teach us of His ways."

In HAGGAI, *the second chapter*, God declares,— "Yet once, it is a little while, and I will shake the heavens, and the earth, and the sea, and the dry land; and I will shake all nations, and the DESIRE

OF ALL NATIONS shall come; and I will fill this
House with glory, saith the Lord of Hosts . . . . *The
glory of this latter House shall be greater than the
former*, saith the Lord of Hosts: and in this place
will I give peace, saith the Lord of Hosts." Surely
this was only, as it were, *typically* fulfilled by the
first coming of the Lord. A more perfect accomplishment is demanded by the prophet's language.

ZECHARIAH also speaks very plainly, not only in
the passage we have already quoted, which declares
that "the man whose name is THE BRANCH . . . .
shall build the Temple," but also in the *last chapter*
of his prophecy, where he declares the judgment
against all the families of the earth, which "go not
up from year to year to worship the King, the Lord
of Hosts" at Jerusalem, and "to keep the feast of
Tabernacles." And where also he says "in that day
shall there be upon the bells of the horses, Holiness
unto the Lord; and the pots *in the Lord's House*
shall be like the bowls before the Altar. Yea, every
pot in Jerusalem, and in Judah, shall be Holiness
unto the Lord of Hosts; and *all they that sacrifice*,
shall come and take of them, and seethe therein: and
in that day there shall be no more the Canaanite
in the House of the Lord of Hosts."

Such is the testimony which it has pleased God
to afford respecting the Millennial Temple and the
Services thereof. We find that EZEKIEL does not
stand by any means without support. To him, indeed was committed the *accurate description;*—but
other prophets were to add corroborative testimony,
more or less powerful. And now may we not ask

with confidence, WHO ART THOU THAT REPLIEST AGAINST GOD?" Nay, *let not poor erring man* REPLY, but wait, depending with a simple confidence upon what the Lord has said, till he behold more clearly than EZEKIEL in the vision, the vast glory of the King of Kings, and rejoice with all His people in the complete display of those transcendent wonders of His love and power, which will be certainly revealed before the eyes of all whose hearts shall be prepared to render hallowed praise and join the angels in their blissful adoration.

In such an aspect, O how great and glorious does the *day of Israel's rest* appear! How wonderfully honored and how richly blest! Their King reigning in unspotted righteousness; their Princes executing perfect judgment; their Priests and Levites carrying out the will of God in truth;—the presence of the Lord, himself, also, among them; His glory filling all His House, and declaring it to be—"THE PLACE OF MY THRONE, AND THE PLACE OF THE SOLES OF MY FEET, WHERE I WILL DWELL IN THE MIDST OF THE CHILDREN OF ISRAEL FOR EVER," and adding "AND MY HOLY NAME SHALL THE HOUSE OF ISRAEL NO MORE DEFILE."*

And how happy also the condition of ALL NATIONS. Their swords beaten into plowshares and their spears into pruning-hooks. No warfare learned. Peace everywhere. The knowledge of God's glory in every family. No man finding need to say to any Brother, "Know the Lord," because all shall know Him from the least to the greatest. O what

* Ezekiel xliii. 7.

a glorious change from that which we are called to witness now!! Should we not then pray with increased earnestness—"THY KINGDOM COME"?

So, for the predicted period of ONE THOUSAND YEARS shall the Redeemer's kingdom on the earth endure in undisturbed righteousness and peace. Yet this shall be but, as it were, the entrance gate of a more glorious period of His reign:—for "OF THE INCREASE OF HIS GOVERNMENT AND PEACE THERE SHALL BE NO END, UPON THE THRONE OF DAVID, AND UPON HIS KINGDOM, TO ORDER IT, AND TO ESTABLISH IT, WITH JUDGMENT, AND WITH JUSTICE, FROM HENCEFORTH EVEN FOR EVER."

CHAPTER VII.

THE FINAL OUTBREAK OF EVIL.

"Thus saith the Lord God, It shall also come to pass that at the same time shall things come into thy mind, and thou shalt think an evil thought: and thou shalt say I will go up to the land of unwalled villages; I will go to them that are at rest, that dwell safely, all of them dwelling without walls, and having neither bars nor gates, to take a spoil, and to take a prey."—EZEKIEL xxxviii. 10—12.

THE LORD'S GREAT DAY, so rich in righteousness and peace, will (as we have seen) endure in its MERIDIAN SPLENDOR for "A THOUSAND YEARS." During this long period the world is to enjoy rest indeed. The day which dawned in fearful judgment, shall find good reason to rejoice because of universal piety—and undisturbed repose beneath Immanuel's sceptre. But the EVENING of this great and glorious Day must follow; for this world is not designed to be our everlasting home. Therefore the deep shadows which foretell approaching night, will be extended over all things earthly.

THE EVENING OF THE LORD'S GREAT DAY will afford subjects which are to occupy both this and the succeeding chapters.

In dwelling on the peculiar features of the Saviour's Reign of Peace, we were careful, I trust, to observe that, although the Word of God has said so much concerning the extent to which true righteousness will prevail, yet it has revealed with perfect clearness, that *the sinful nature of the fallen Adam will remain, so that there will be a tendency to do evil, as great as that which exists now.* But inasmuch as Satan will be bound, and suffered to deceive mankind no longer, this tendency will be deprived of its most powerful instigator; and since faith will be in measure lost in sight, and incentives to perform the Will of God, will, in a peculiar manner be presented to the eye of man, *the fleshly power of evil will be in great measure latent.* None perhaps will be able to charge the converted people of the Lord with inconsistency; and those who may remain yet unregenerate, will walk *orderly* before the eyes of men. But all will be in readiness, so that if the Adversary should again be free from his imprisonment, sin would be aroused at once, and the whole world again would lie in wickedness. Thus sin and sinners would assume their old position, and peace would have the prominence no more, except, of course, the Lord were to be pleased to pour forth an amount of His constraining grace which hitherto has not been granted to the world.

Now, we are told in the *twentieth chapter* of REVELATION that "when the thousand years are expired, Satan shall be loosed out of prison, and shall go out to deceive the nations." So then, it shall be. As, for want of any explanation being granted in the inspired word, we did not pause to ask what was meant by Satan being bound and cast into the bottomless pit; so, for the same reason, we will not stay to make inquiry as to his release therefrom. Let it suffice; he shall again walk to and fro in this world, seeking whom he may *sift* and whom he may *devour.* The "LIAR," the "ACCUSER," the "DECEIVER" still, he will immediately prove himself to be. To over-throw the kingdom of the Lord, to engulf the souls of men in everlasting ruin, to spread sin and misery around, will be, as they have ever been, the base of his designs. So, he "shall go out to deceive the nations," and, as in all former time, he shall too well succeed.

What period will be allowed for this renewed attempt against the Lord's dominion is not stated, but, from the particulars which are given of the work of evil to be carried on, there is good reason to believe it will be *brief.*

Let us now carefully examine what is said concern-ing the sad work which Satan will perform.

Two verses only of the chapter to which we just referred (*the twentieth of* REVELATION) have described it. They tell us that Satan "shall go out to deceive the nations which are in the four quarters of the earth, Gog and Magog, to gather them together to battle: the number of whom is as the sand of the sea. And they went up on the breadth of the earth, and compassed the camp of the Saints about, and the be-loved city." Certainly it appears by this that Satan will put forth much energy: and that he and his legions will be *everywhere* at work. The expression "*the four quarters of the earth*" appears to leave no land excepted; but to intimate that wheresoever there are people to be tempted, there the tempter's hand will be outstretched.

From the chapter now under our consideration we can obtain very little distinct information as to the extent or power of the last outbreak. But this is not the only place in Scripture in which this last display of sin is spoken of. We find it brought forward also, and far more explicitly, by EZEKIEL. This prophet—having spoken, in the *thirty-seventh chapter*, of the restoration of Israel, and of the blessings of the reign of David under the new covenant of peace, on which we dwelt particularly in our last chapter,—introduces a new subject in the *thirty-eighth chapter;* a subject quite inconsistent with the reign of quietness and holy calm which is to mark that happy age. It reads as follows:—"The word of the Lord came unto me, saying, Son of Man, set thy face against GOG, the land of MAGOG, the Chief Prince of Meshech and Tubal, and prophesy against him, and say, thus saith the Lord God, Behold, I am against thee, O GOG, the Chief Prince of Meshech and Tubal: And I will turn thee back, and put hooks into thy jaws, and I will bring thee forth, and all thine army, horses, and horsemen, all of them clothed with all sorts of armor, even a great company with buckles and shields, all of them handling swords: PERSIA, ETHIOPIA, and LIBYA with them; all of them with shield and helmet: GOMER, and all his bands; the house of TOGARMAH of the NORTH QUARTERS, and all his bands; and many people with thee. Be thou prepared, and prepare for thyself, thou, and all thy company that are assembled unto thee, and be thou a guard unto them. *After many days thou shalt be visited;* IN THE LATTER YEARS *thou shalt come into the land that is brought back from the sword, and is gathered out of many people, against the mountains of Israel,* which have been always waste: BUT IT IS BROUGHT FORTH OUT OF THE NATIONS, AND THEY SHALL DWELL SAFELY ALL OF THEM. Thou shalt *ascend* and *come like a storm;* thou shalt be like a cloud to cover the land, thou and all thy bands, and many people with thee. Thus saith the Lord God, It shall also come to pass, that at the same time shall things come into thy mind, and thou shalt think an evil thought; and thou shalt say, I will go up to the land of UNWALLED VILLAGES; I will go to THEM THAT ARE AT REST, THAT DWELL SAFELY, ALL OF THEM DWELLING WITHOUT WALLS, AND HAVING NEITHER BARS NOR GATES, to take a spoil, and to take a prey; to turn thine hand upon the desolate places that are now inhabited, and upon the people that are gathered out of the nations, which have gotten cattle and goods, that dwell in the midst of the land. SHEBA and DEDAN, and the MERCHANTS OF TARSHISH, with all the young lions thereof, shall say unto thee, Art thou come to take a spoil? Hast thou gathered thy company to take a prey, to carry away silver and gold, to take away cattle and goods, to take a great spoil? Therefore, Son of Man, prophesy and say unto GOG, Thus saith the Lord God, In that day, when my people of Israel dwelleth safely, shalt thou not know it? And thou shalt come from thy place OUT OF THE NORTH PARTS, thou, and many people with thee, all of them riding upon horses, a great company, and a mighty army: And thou shalt come up *against my people of Israel as a cloud to cover the land;* IT SHALL BE IN THE LATTER DAYS."

12

Now in this passage which I have quoted at length, we find ISRAEL dwelling *securely* in "unwalled villages," having "neither bars nor gates." Israel, thus secure, is spoken of, as "brought back from the sword," and gathered out of many people." It would appear also that certain nations will be associated in close friendship with Israel, when GOG shall stand up against them. Among these are mentioned SHEBA, DEDAN, and TARSHISH. While in league with GOG, against God's people, will be PERSIA, ETHIOPIA, LIBYA, GOMER, and TOGARMAH. That is to say, that when the power of Satan is again allowed to be exerted over the minds of men, very few by comparison will stand firmly on the Lord's side, even though there be in Israel the clearest evidence that He is King indeed, and though His manifested power and justice are beyond the reach of question. But let us examine this, that we may learn something, if it may be, of the power which Gog will be permitted to exercise in the world, as well as of the standing which Israel will take, and the success they will meet with, when the land shall be besieged by the last overwhelming army.

We will speak first of ISRAEL and THEIR ALLIES in the day of the great siege.

I need not call your attention again to the territory which Israel will possess: that great peninsula* with its arid deserts rejoicing and blossoming as the rose, its howling wilderness turned into so many fruitful fields, its people happy in a "quietness and assurance" which the experience of a thousand years

* See Chapter III., page 51.

will have taught them to regard as their unceasing portion. But of the nations which are named as Israel's allies, we may do well to speak particularly. Referring to the passage we have quoted from EZEKIEL, we find that these allies of the Lord's people will be *three*—SHEBA, DEDAN, and TARSHISH.

SHEBA, which is the first mentioned, is said by Josephus to be "Egypt and Ethiopia."* But there are good reasons for considering Josephus to have been mistaken: though it is possible (and the annals of Ethiopia referred to by Bruce, confirm it) that the famous Queen of Sheba had dominions in that country. Indeed our Saviour says that this Queen was "the Queen of the SOUTH," and "came from THE UTTERMOST PARTS OF THE EARTH." Now this might be properly asserted, if she came from the *Arabian* banks of the Red Sea,—but *not* if she came from *Ethiopia*,—as a reference to a map will show plainly. Moreover, there is good reason for supposing that although (according to Major Scott Phillips and others) a considerable tract of land on the east of the Red Sea, about one thousand miles in length by an average of three hundred wide, will not be appropriated to any of the tribes of Israel, yet that it will be occupied by nations subject to the king of Israel's sovereignty. *Border States ministering to the wants of the twelve tribes.* There, perhaps, KEDAR will be in readiness to supply servants.† There NEBAIOTH will make folds for flocks.‡ There SEBA will cultivate her land and reap abun-

---

* Antiq. Book viii. Chap. vi. s. 5.

† Isaiah lx. 7.   ‡ Isaiah lx. 7.

dance, that she may offer gifts.* And there SHEBA too, having the "SOUTH" lands, will dig her mines, and heap her stores of gold, and gather incense for the Temple of a GREATER KING that he whose wisdom in the days of old amazed her Queen.†

The second place mentioned is DEDAN. This seems to be a tract of land about five hundred miles in length and of uncertain width (probably, about one hundred miles), occupying the extremity of the land of Arabia, having the Persian Gulf on the north-west and north-east. A country well fitted for the occupation of those who should serve Israel with the merchandise of India.

Then as to TARSHISH.—"The *Merchants*" thereof only are spoken of. Hence we may at once conclude that wherever Tarshish may be situated, it is a *mercantile country*. But of what country *at the present time* are *merchants* in such proximity to Arabia (the future land of Israel) as to warrant a reference to *them*, as the men who will rise up and stand by God's people when they shall be suddenly besieged by Satan's multitudes? I think our eyes will either pass immediately across the sea *eastward* from DEDAN till we arrive at India: or they will look *northward* to the shores of "THE GREAT SEA"—the MEDITERRANEAN. But, in either case, the sought for *merchants* which would more especially attract attention from all nations in the days in which we live, are those pertaining to the people who hold GIBRALTAR,—"the key of the Mediterranean:" for at, or close to, this important stronghold, (not far-

* Psalm lxxii. 10.   † Isaiah lx. 6.

ther, certainly, than the mouth of the Guadalquiver) was the famous TARTESSUS of the ancients, which, as almost all good commentators are agreed, was the TARSHISH of Scripture, associated so constantly and closely with "The Isles."*

OUR OWN DEAR ENGLAND, then, (there is some ground to *hope*) may be a nation which God has prepared to stand by those who are, by a peculiar choice, HIS PEOPLE, even to the last.

But there is another matter which adds strength to this most acceptable ground of hope. England is said to have been twice colonized by the descendants of TARSHISH the son of Javan; viz., by the Tyrians and the Carthaginians, agreeably indeed to the declaration—"And the Sons of Javan; Elishah, Tarshish, Kittim, and Dodanim. By these were the Isles of the Gentiles divided."† A declaration which may fairly be viewed as a prophecy.

When therefore "THE MERCHANTS OF TARSHISH" are spoken of, it will not be considered that we form an opinion foolishly, if we suppose that the people of our own beloved country, who, for purposes of trade, inhabit our Indian Colonies, may be intended. Nor shall we be thought to reason groundlessly, if we argue favorably with regard to the stability of our British Empire, even when so many nations of the earth will be shaken to their everlasting overthrow.

But if there be indeed a basis for an expectation so happy, then let our Christian fellow-countrymen remember, that TARSHISH is to be *severely chastened*

---

* Psalm lxxii. 10. Isaiah xxiii. 1, 2 & 6. Isaiah lx. 9. &c. &c.
† Genesis x. 4—5.

(although not destroyed) before the dawn of the Millennial peace.* God will chastise her with a rod of bitterness, although in love, and from the burden of her chastisement she will arise and shine in glory, and be well prepared to stand in all the greatness of her strength, when in the latest hour of this world's Evening, SIN BREAKS FORTH WITH SUCH EXCEEDING MIGHT.

Thus far then for the nations which in the last outburst of evil, shall stand firmly as *the friends of Israel.*

Now let us observe also the *other* nations, which will gather under the banner of the deceived monarch GOG. They are PERSIA, ETHIOPIA, LIBYA, GOMER, and TOGARMAH.

Concerning these countries also, we may be allowed to occupy a few moments in referring to their situation and extent. Of GOG and MAGOG we will speak afterwards.

As to PERSIA, we need only point to any map of Asia, and call to mind the capabilities which that vast country once displayed, and may display again, for obtaining power and greatness.

ETHIOPIA, if we are to comprehend beneath that name the whole of the "Ethiopia Interior" of the ancients,—will reach from East to West of Africa, having the "Mountains of the Moon" on the South.

LIBYA, also, if we are to include "Libya" proper, "Libya Deserta," and "Libya Interior," stretches from Egypt, north of "Ethiopia Interior," to the extreme West.

* Isaiah ii. 16. Isaiah xxiii. 1 and 6.

The situation and extent of GOMER are not so easily determined. GOMER was the eldest son of Japheth.* It is said that his descendants peopled a considerable part of Asia Minor. From thence they emigrated, till Germany, Gaul, and perhaps some portions of more northerly countries were occupied by them. In fact it is supposed that the Cimmerii, Cimbri, Cumbri, Umbri, Cambri, and others, were but names of different tribes of Gomer, which spread themselves from the Black Sea to the Atlantic, and from the shores of the Baltic to Italy, the additional names of Celts, Gauls, Galatæ, and Gaels, being given to them.* Whether this be correct or not, thus far appears probable,—That the descendants of Gomer *did* spread themselves over a great part of Southern Europe, including FRANCE and GERMANY. It seems then that in GOMER we have the representative of all the great European powers, England perhaps excepted, united in support of GOG.

But what of TOGARMAH? He was the third son of GOMER.† The majority of learned men appear to be of opinion that the children of Togarmah peopled the regions of Armenia, Cappadocia, and Phrygia.

But now if it be so, and we combine Persia, Ethiopia, Libya, Gomer, and Togarmah, what a *vast strength* we find prepared to side with GOG. From India to the West of Europe, and from the Mountains of the Moon to the Baltic, if not farther northward still, shall those apostatizing nations be, which will take part against the people of the Lord.

But we must say a word concerning their great

---

* Genesis x. 2.   * See Calmet.   † Genesis x. 3.

leaders—GOG and MAGOG. Now the chapter from
which we have drawn the conclusion just stated, viz.,
the *thirty-eighth* of EZEKIEL, speaks thus—"And the
word of the Lord came unto me, saying, Son of Man,
set thy face against GOG, the land of MAGOG, the
chief prince of Meshech and Tubal, and prophesy
against him: And say, thus saith the Lord God, behold I am against thee, O Gog, the chief prince
of Meshech and Tubal." Now the meaning of this
passage as it stands thus, is by no means evident.
But perhaps we can throw a little light upon it by
reference to the Septuagint translation, where it
stands as follows: " Καὶ ἐγένετο λογος, κυριου προς με
. . . . . στηρισον το προσωπον σου ἐπι Γωγ, και την γῆν
του Μαγωγ, ἀρχοντα ῾Ρως, Μεσοχ, και Θοβελ, ...
και εἰπον αυτῷ . . . . . . ἰδου εγω ἐπι σε ἀρχοντα ῾Ρως,
Μεσοχ, και Θοβελ."—which in English would read as
follows:—"And a word of the Lord came unto me
. . . . . . set thy face against GOG and the land of
Magog, prince of Rhos, Mesoch, and Thobel . . . . .
and say to him . . . . . . Behold I (am) against thee,
prince of Rhos, Mesoch and Thobel." Now if this
rendering be received, and GOG inhabiting the land
of MAGOG, be the Prince of Rhos, Mesoch, and
Thobel,* there is but little difficulty in arriving at a
conclusion probably correct.

MAGOG, a son of Japheth, is generally believed to
have been the father of the SCYTHIANS and TAR-

---

* That Gog, not Magog, is the prince of Rosh, Mesoch, and
Thobel, is proved by reference to chapter xxxix. 1, where we read,
"Behold I am against thee, O Gog, the chief prince (or rather the
prince of Rosh) of Mesech and Tubal."

TARS; and the TARTARS and MUSCOVITES possess the
territories which belonged in ancient time to the
SCYTHIANS,—and retain several traces of the names
"GOG and MAGOG."* Therefore we may deem it,
at least, probable, that Gog, the prince of Rosh
(רֹאשׁ), or Rhos ('Pως) is in fact the prince who shall
have sway in that vast country we call RUSSIA.
Nay, this surely becomes almost more than probability, when we couple Mesech (or Mesoch) and
Tubal (or Thobel) with Rosh (or Rhos;) for if we
bear in mind that *ou*, and *sk* are terminations peculiar to the Sclavonic languages, we find MESOCH and
THOBEL more nearly allied than perhaps we had
expected, to Moscow and TOBOLSK. Now RUSSIA,
MOSCOW, and TOBOLSK were in old time the three
subdivisions of the RUSSIAN EMPIRE. Who then is
more likely to be the GOG here spoken of, than he
who in the last hour of this earth's eventide, shall
have dominion over RUSSIA? And what country is
more likely than RUSSIA—*the Scythian's land*—to
prove itself "THE LAND OF MAGOG?"

So then we have shown that the nations which
shall be confederate against Israel at the time of
which we speak, will be many, great, and powerful.
And those who still adhere to her as firm allies, will
be but *few*, and for the more part *weak*. TARSHISH
being the only great and independent nation spoken
of, and of Tarshish, the whole people not being
brought forward, but "the merchants" and "*the
young lions*" thereof, ONLY.

Thus, when Satan shall be loosed out of his prison,

* See Calmet.

he will go out to deceive the nations; and with a *vast multitude* of people he will have success. And these, led on by GOG—whom SATAN will empower as he did *Antichrist* a thousand years before—will "think an evil thought; and will come up "to take a spoil and to take a prey" from the land of riches and of peace.

Now it is declared in the brief prophecy of this outbreak in the *twentieth chapter* of the REVELATION, that the nations "went up on the breadth of the earth, and compassed the camp of the saints round about, and the beloved city." This passage brings us to the point at which the armies are assembled, on the eve of carrying out the grand object of their union. All things are ready: the munitions of war are complete: and the armies of the wicked nations are prepared to go up "*on the breadth of the earth.*" It does not at first sight appear at all evident what is intended by this expression, "*the breadth of the earth.*" It may be worthy of examination. It stands thus in the original: "*και ανεβησαν επι το πλατος της γης:*" which may be translated thus,— *And they mounted upon the broad place of the land.* Now, undoubtedly, "the land," the possession of which is to be the grand object of this unholy confederacy, is THE LAND OF ISRAEL.* And the particular point of the combined attack is to be JERUSALEM, "THE BELOVED CITY."† But in order to besiege Jerusalem, in the situation which it will occupy in the Millennial age, it will be necessary to *mount the height of that exalted plain,* which will reach (as I endeavored to show in the last chapter,) from Geba

* Ezekiel xxxviii.   † Revelation xx. 9.

to Rimmon, and from the Mediterranean to the Dead Sea; that is to say, about *sixty miles square.* This I conceive to be "*the breadth of the earth,*" or "*the broad place of the land,*" on which it is declared they shall "*go up.*" Here, no doubt, the mighty armies of the confederate nations, the allies of Gog, will be assembled, and will lay siege against "the camp of the saints, and the beloved city."

And now that they have prepared all for the attack, and "Sheba, Dedan, and the Merchants of Tarshish, with all the young lions thereof," have uttered their remonstrance—"Art thou come to take a spoil? Hast thou gathered thy company to take a prey? To carry away silver and gold, to take away cattle and goods, to take a great spoil?"—Then it will be immediately the work of God Himself to stand up on behalf of Israel. There will be no battle fought. No scaling engine will be raised. No sword effectually drawn against the servants of the Lord. But He will raise His own Almighty arm, and He will work and none shall let it.—So, when it is declared in the brief record given us in the Book of Revelation—"And they went up on the breadth of the earth, and compassed the Camp of the Saints about, and the beloved City:" we find this further declaration,—"And fire came down from God out of Heaven, and devoured them."

But we shall again find details in the same chapter of Ezekiel, we before referred to—*the thirty-eighth,* commencing with the *eighteenth verse,*—"And it shall come to pass at the same time when Gog shall come against the land of Israel, saith the Lord God, that my fury shall come up in my face. For in my jealousy, and in the fire of my wrath, have I spoken, Surely in that day there shall be a great shaking in the land of Israel; so that the fishes of the sea, and the fowls of heaven, and the beasts of the field, and all creeping things that creep upon the earth, and all the men that are upon the face of the earth, shall shake AT MY PRESENCE; and the mountains shall be thrown down, and the steep places shall fall, and every wall shall fall to the ground. And I will call for a sword against him throughout all my mountains, saith the Lord God: *Every man's sword shall be against his brother. And I will plead against him with pestilence and with blood; and I will rain upon him, and upon his bands, and upon the many people that are with him, an overflowing rain, and great hailstones, fire and brimstone.*"*

It seems, then, that when the nations are assembled on the great plain of Jerusalem, compassing the city round about for an immediate attack,—THE LORD SHALL APPEAR as the defender of his people: fear and trembling will fall upon the nations: the sword of Israel will be called for: and in the confederate camp there will be slaughter, brother against brother, as in the days of Gideon† and of Jonathan.‡

---

* It may be right to note that it appears to me that with this 38th chapter of Ezekiel the most distant point in the prophecy is arrived at. The next chapter still deals with Gog and Magog, but commences a fresh prophecy concerning them, having for its period of fulfilment the time immediately *preceding* the restoration of Israel and the erection of the Millennial Temple. A careful perusal of the 39th chapter will, I think, place this beyond doubt.

† Judges vii. 22.   ‡ 1 Samuel xiv. 15, 20.

Moreover the Lord will plead with PESTILENCE; like that, perhaps, which is described by ZECHARIAH thus—"Their flesh shall consume away while they stand upon their feet, and their eyes shall consume away in their holes, and their tongue shall consume away in their mouth. . . . . And so shall be the plague of the horse, of the mule, of the camel, and of the ass, and of all the beasts that shall be in their tent, as this plague."* And he will also plead with BLOOD; for the slaughter shall be very great, because "it shall come to pass in that day that a great tumult from the Lord shall be among them; and they shall lay hold every one on the hand of his neighbor, and his hand shall rise up against the hand of his neighbor. And Judah also shall fight at Jerusalem."† Nor is this all; for the Lord will plead with FIRE; for He will rain upon GOG and upon his bands, and upon the many people that are with him, GREAT HAIL-STONES, FIRE AND BRIMSTONE; YEA, FIRE SHALL COME DOWN FROM GOD OUT OF HEAVEN, AND DEVOUR THEM.

So shall the last outbreak of iniquity be silenced, and its power destroyed. It would appear that no *effectual* blow will be struck against God's people. He whom they have served will keep them safely, and not a hair of their head shall perish.

But now the time will have arrived, not only for the punishment of SINNERS, but also for the effectual rooting out of SIN. And so we read that the DEVIL that deceived the nations will be "cast into the LAKE OF FIRE AND BRIMSTONE, where the BEAST and the

* Zechariah xiv. 12—15.
† Compare Ezekiel xxxviii. 21, with Zechariah xiv. 13, 14.

FALSE PROPHET are, and shall be tormented day and night for ever and ever."* He is not *now* to be bound in prison for a certain period, whence again he may go forth and re-commence his work of evil, but he is to be cast into HELL, INTO THE FIRE THAT NEVER SHALL BE QUENCHED, that there, in torment, day and night, he may, beyond the reach of any whom he might excite to sin, endure for all eternity the fearful penalty his works deserve.

Thus SATAN,—the great prince of darkness,—the author of man's sin and misery,—who for all ages of the world has labored to uproot the work of God, and to eradicate all virtue, and all peace, and to overthrow eternally the kingdom of the Lord of lords,—will pass from the presence of God's children, leaving HIM "WHOSE RIGHT IT IS," to reign in undisturbed possession; leaving ISRAEL in peace; leaving EVERY SAINT unscathed; *not having taken one believing, praying soul of man, since Adam fell, from the protecting arm of God;* nay, leaving vividly on record, that the praises of the everlasting age might dwell upon it in the blissful harmony of Heaven, "WHERE SIN ABOUNDED GRACE DID MUCH MORE ABOUND: THAT AS SIN HATH REIGNED UNTO DEATH, EVEN SO MIGHT GRACE REIGN, THROUGH RIGHTEOUSNESS, UNTO ETERNAL LIFE, BY JESUS CHRIST OUR LORD."

* Revelation xx. 10.

CHAPTER VIII.

LAST RESURRECTION AND JUDGMENT.

"Out of Zion the perfection of beauty, God hath shined. Our God shall come, and shall not keep silence; a fire shall devour before Him, and it shall be very tempestuous round about him. He shall call to the heavens from above, and to the earth, that He may judge His people."—PSALM l. 2—4.

WE have already dwelt upon the probability that THE LAST OUTBREAK OF WICKEDNESS will be *very brief;* its fury being cut short by the tremendous stroke of the Almighty arm. But the crowning effort of the Wicked One, being thus turned into foolishness, all things will be ready for the ONE REMAINING SCENE which is to mark the close of EARTH'S EVENTFUL EVENTIDE, and introduce again the darkness, which in the primeval days dwelt "on the face of the deep."

That ONE REMAINING SCENE is now to come before us for consideration.

Not *every* eye will feast upon the glories of the Reign of Peace, nor behold the Tabernacle of the Lord with men. Not every heart will swell with rapture at the blessedness of the Millennial inheritance, nor join the praises which from multitudes out of all nations will ascend acceptably to the Eternal Father's throne. But now that the Millennial reign is passed, and Satan is secured in the eternal prison-house, whence there is no return; the day is come for God Almighty to be "All in All."* AN EVERLAST-ING END MUST BE PUT ONCE FOR ALL TO SIN, AND THE DESERTS OF EVERY MAN AND EVERY DEVIL, EVERLAST-INGLY AWARDED. *Every eye*, therefore, must now behold, and *every heart* be roused to confidence or dread.

For this, THE TRUMPET, long foretold, will give forth its awakening blast; the VOICE OF THE ETERNAL SON OF GOD be uttered with Almighty strength; the vast depths of earth and sea be penetrated; the continents and isles attend. And "in a moment, in the twinkling of an eye," will all THE DEAD GIVE HEED; the dead of yesterday—the dead of ages past. *Their* ashes, for whom tears have just begun to flow, and *theirs* whose names have, for revolving centuries, been buried in oblivion. All these shall *hear*, and *heed*, and RISE. Their old corruption put on incorruption, and their mortal, immortality. Before the Trumpet-blast and the almighty voice go forth, their bodies abode silently beneath the earth or in the ocean depths; enshrined securely and at rest; but when the Trumpet and the Voice have sounded, it is otherwise. ONE MOMENT ONLY, and the surface of the earth and sea is covered with a multitude no man can number;—the dead who in all ages and all nations have departed, *but are not in Christ*—the dead of this world's people who have left their earthly life *unpardoned* and *unsaved.*—These dead come forth, and stand prepared for judgment.

* Corinthians xv. 28.

Now, it would appear that when these have arisen, EARTH itself, untenanted by the remains of any son of Adam, will receive its portion of the judgment, for the sin with which, since the primeval fall, it has been stained.

Raised high, in sight of all, will be the GREAT WHITE THRONE; and on the seat thereof, the SON OF MAN, arrayed in the eternal glory of the Father, will hold session. From the brightness of his face all nature will shrink back. The heaven and the earth will flee away, and no place be found for them.* The judgment of Almighty God will overtake them, and they must pay the penalty of sin, according to the word of prophecy,—"The heavens shall pass away with a great noise, and the elements shall melt with fervent heat; the earth also, and the works that are therein, shall be burned up . . . . . the heavens, being on fire, shall be dissolved, and the elements shall melt with fervent heat."† *How* this shall be, we know not. That it *will be*, is certain, as the word of God is true. But when the earth, and heaven which surrounds the earth, have passed away in fire from the exceeding glory of the King of Kings,— "the dead both small and great" are to be summoned to the Throne. And they will obey. It is not now to be as on a former day, that the Lord will send His angels to gather His Elect from the four winds, from one end of *heaven* to the other;—but that He will send them to constrain the multitudes of the *unsaved* who have arisen from the tomb, the grave, the sea, that they ascend and gather *on the left hand of the*

* Revelation xx. 11.   † 2 Peter iii. 10—12.

13

great Throne, that He who sits thereon may bring their deeds to light, and judge them in His righteousness. From this assembly not one soul of the last risen dead will be excepted. Every man, every woman, every child, will be there. The rich, the poor, the learned, the ignorant, will be there. And how all faces will have gathered blackness! Not one gleam of hope,—but everywhere the darkness of despair.

These might have served God and so inherited salvation *if they would: but they would not.* The door of grace was opened wide for them, and was kept open long, but they refused to enter. What will they then advance against the Lord, when He, in *very justice*, shall have closed the door and bid them stand without?

But here I pause an instant, lest among my readers there be any who have lived regardless of their day of grace. O let me speak a faithful word to them. It is a very little while, before both you and I must leave this world that we may stand before the Lord. As the tree falls, so it must lie. As we die, so we must abide until the day of resurrection. God gives us all a day of grace, wherein are ample opportunities granted us for turning to Him and obtaining sure acceptance. No one of us can stand up against God, and say that opportunities have been denied him,— for Christ Jesus has made full atonement for the sins *of all*, and God will give His Holy Spirit to all those who ask Him, that they may believe on the Lord Jesus Christ, and live. If any sinner *will believe*, he *may believe;* and to believe is to be *justified* and

SAVED. I would ask each of my readers to weigh carefully the following passages, and then to ask himself,—CAN I ESCAPE IF I NEGLECT SO GREAT SALVATION? Jesus said, "As Moses lifted up the serpent in the wilderness, even so must the SON OF MAN be lifted up, that WHOSOEVER BELIEVETH ON HIM, SHOULD NOT PERISH, BUT HAVE EVERLASTING LIFE."* Jesus said again, "VERILY, VERILY, I SAY UNTO YOU, HE THAT BELIEVETH ON ME *HATH* EVERLASTING LIFE."† *O is not the way of our salvation plain?* What poor sinner need perish? What anxious, burdened soul, need go unpardoned. As the serpent-bitten Children of Israel did but LOOK upon the brazen image Moses reared, and received HEALING *instantly*, however deep the wound, however far the venom had penetrated the system; so may the conscience-stricken sinner, who is bitten by the Serpent which deceived Eve, and in whose soul the poison of iniquity has been effecting its sure work of death,—look up to Jesus Christ,—look up to Him *with confidence*, and live. No burdened soul which looks on him with faith can perish. The weakest of believers on the Son of God shall have a glorious never-failing portion in the Saint's inheritance. WHO THEN SHALL ESCAPE IF HE NEGLECT SO GREAT SALVATION, ATTAINABLE MOREOVER BY SUCH VERY SIMPLE MEANS?

But now to return. We leave the wicked gathered in despair on the left hand of the Almighty Judge

* John iii. 14, 15. Read also verses 16—18 and 36.
† John vi. 47. See also Acts xvi. 31, Romans v. 1, and x. 8, 9, &c., &c.

to contemplate another company:—THE RIGHTEOUS. All these likewise are gathered. Not one soul of them is wanting. They stand upon *the right*. Already these have known the King, for they have shared with him the government of the Millennial Kingdom, or else have been therein, His earthly subjects. They have known that they are saved. They have known that condemnation cannot be the portion of the weakest soul among them. But they stand there *to endure the judgment*, and a strict all-searching scrutiny they must submit to. They have built, indeed, by grace, on THE FOUNDATION GOD HAS LAID, and THEY ARE SAFE, though heaven and earth shall pass away. Now *some* of them have built with GOLD, some with SILVER, some with PRECIOUS STONES, on this foundation. Each of these will stand the test of the devouring flame with greater or less firmness. But *others* have built only WOOD, or HAY, or STUBBLE, which the devouring flame will speedily consume.

As these Redeemed ones stand there before the Lord, the fire of His all-searching justice will effectually try the work of every man, *to prove it, of what sort it is;* and if, thus being tested by the fire, the work of any man abide which he has built, *he shall receive reward accordingly*. But if any man's work be burned, he shall *suffer loss:* yet "HE HIMSELF SHALL BE SAVED;" although it may be *just* saved—"so as by fire."*

Thus then without a fear of condemnation, but awaiting an unerring sentence, will the righteous stand before the Judge of All.

* 1 Corinthians iii. 11—15.

But now, one word on their condition. We have called them "RIGHTEOUS." Truly so: for "*righteous*" is their fitting title. Christ himself has called them so.*

Shall I be thought to assert that which *is not*, if I say that the weakest of believers,—though his life may have been *vile with sin* before he came to Christ with faith,—is already *perfectly righteous* before God. From that moment in which he believed in Jesus Christ, and trusted his immortal soul implicitly to Him, he is not only *forgiven*, not only *saved*, but he is ACTUALLY RIGHTEOUS in the sight of Heaven. But an assertion such as this must not be allowed to pass unproved. Let us inquire concerning it in the Word of God. The grand truths which are so patent in the Bible, viz., that the Lord hath laid on Christ the iniquity of us all; that Christ hath borne our griefs and carried our sorrows; that by His stripes we are healed; that we have pardon and remission of sins through His blood, which cleanseth from all sin: are comforting indeed to the sincere believer. But they form a *part* only of the great treasure which God's hand hold's forth for the acceptance of the anxious soul. The believer in Christ Jesus, is not only washed in His atoning blood: he is not only rendered clean, the guilt and filthiness of his transgressions being taken from him, but he is *justified* also; he is *clothed upon*, as it were, with RIGHTEOUSNESS which is *not his own*, nor has been wrought by any *creature* in the universe; even the RIGHTEOUSNESS OF CHRIST,

* Matthew xiii. 43, xxv. 46.

which is the RIGHTOUSNESS OF GOD.* See, now, how unmistakably the Apostle Paul dwells upon this in the *third chapter* of his Epistle to the ROMANS. Having declared the fact that "All the world" is "guilty before God," and that "By the deeds of the law there shall no flesh be justified in his sight;" he adds—"But now THE RIGHTEOUSNESS OF GOD without the law, is manifested, being witnessed by the law and the prophets: even THE RIGHTEOUS-NESS OF GOD WHICH IS BY FAITH OF JESUS CHRIST, UNTO ALL AND UPON ALL THEM THAT BELIEVE: FOR THERE IS NO DIFFERENCE: for all have sinned and come short of the glory of God; BEING JUSTIFIED FREELY BY HIS GRACE THROUGH THE REDEMPTION THAT IS IN CHRIST JESUS." What is it then, but that *in the very highest sense,* believers in the Son of God, are entitled to be called "RIGHTEOUS!" And that the rich blessings of the Righteous must be *theirs,* for they are clothed in the very RIGHTEOUSNESS OF GOD! I cannot help referring on this subject to a passage in the writings of the "judicious Hooker;" which speaks very power-fully and with great fulness to the point. He says, "Although in ourselves we be altogether sinful and unrighteous, yet even the man which in himself is impious, full of iniquity, full of sin; him *being found in Christ through faith, and having his sins in hatred through repentance;* him God beholdeth with a gra-cious eye, putteth away his sin by not imputing it, taketh quite away the punishment due thereunto, by

* Jeremiah xxiii. 6. Romans iii. 21—26. 1 Corinthians i. 30—31. 2 Corinthians v. 21, &c.

pardoning it; and accepteth him in Jesus Christ as perfectly righteous, as if he had fulfilled all that is commanded him in the law; *shall I say*, MORE PER- FECTLY RIGHTEOUS *than if himself had fulfilled the whole law?* I must take heed what I say; but *the Apostle* saith,* "God made Him, which knew no sin, *to be sin* for us; that we might be made THE RIGHT- EOUSNESS OF GOD in Him." SUCH WE ARE IN THE SIGHT OF GOD THE FATHER, AS IS THE VERY SON OF GOD HIMSELF. Let it be counted folly, or phrenzy, or fury, or whatsoever. It is our wisdom, and our comfort; we care for no knowledge in the world but this, that man hath sinned, and God hath suffered; that GOD HATH MADE HIMSELF THE SIN OF MEN, AND MEN ARE MADE THE RIGHTEOUSNESS OF GOD." This surely is conclusive. For here we have not Hooker's own peculiar *opinion* given us, but we have the simple, unmistakable assertion of the WORD OF GOD. And we may conclude that all the multitudes of true believers in the Lord Jesus Christ, whether they have passed the stream of death or not, are truly RIGHTEOUS. With every one of them is God well pleased; and righteous in the spotless righteousness of their CREATOR, shall they stand awaiting their reward at the right hand of the Al- mighty Purchaser of their Eternal Bliss. How they will shine forth; how they will express their joy; how they will declare the praises of their great Jehovah-Tsidkenu; we cannot tell. But *this* we know,—they will be LIKE HIM.† They will all be prepared in His unsullied righteousness to reign with

---

* 2 Corinthians v. 21.   † 1 John iii. 2.

Him in an estate more glorious by far than eye of man hath seen, or ear heard, or heart conceived. They shall inherit the kingdom prepared for them from the foundation of the world. They shall go into LIFE ETERNAL.

But let me pause an instant here, that I may speak a word of encouragement to my *fellow-believers*. Is it indeed the case that every one who believes in Jesus Christ is clothed with GOD'S OWN RIGHTEOUS-NESS, and yet so many of us go with *fearing, trembling, doubting* footsteps through this earthly life toward heaven? Why do we thus fear? Why do we thus suffer clouds and darkness to interpose between the Lord and our immortal souls? Why do we not *lay hold* at once of the most glorious hope which is set before us in the gospel? True, true indeed, we have a daily, hourly cause to mourn over our evil habits, our lukewarmness, and our inconsistencies, for "the flesh lusteth against the Spirit and the Spirit against the flesh, and these are contrary the one to the other: so that we cannot do the things that we would."* But though it is so, and by reason of the law of sin in our members, the very best amongst us are too often brought into a sore subjection; yet we need not cry out in despair, "O wretched man that I am, who shall deliver me from the body of this death!" But rather, looking boldly upwards,—behold Jesus, sitting at the right hand of Power, our faithful One,—"The Lord our Righteousness;" and realizing our position through His finished work of love, exclaim,—"I thank my God, through

* Galatians v. 17.

Jesus Christ our Lord."* O how can any true believer find the slightest room for doubt, when it is declared so plainly that he is arrayed in the *pure* RIGHTEOUSNESS OF THE ALL-HOLY GOD! Reader: DOST THOU BELIEVE ON THE SON OF GOD? THEN IT •IS WELL WITH THEE, for thou art RIGHTEOUS, and in righteousness SHALT STAND IN THE GREAT DAY OF CHRIST.

But now turn we from the innumerable multitudes who stand on *one side* or *the other* of the Great White Throne, to meditate upon the ACT OF JUDG-MENT.

Not much is told us in the Word of God concerning this. But quite enough is said to show that it will be a Judgment, wherein *every secret* shall be brought to light, *every life* and *every heart* laid bare, *every thought* and *every word* with accuracy weighed: that nothing shall escape the searching eye of the OMNIS-CIENT JUDGE, nor any soul of man be found unjustly dealt with.

OUR SAVIOUR frequently alluded to the Judgment of mankind, that men might live in constant prepa-ration for it. He spoke of it decidedly, as an act in which each hidden thing shall be made manifest;† in which all men shall give account for every idle word which they have spoken;‡ in which justice shall be done unerringly to every soul of man; he who had received *ten* talents, *five*, or *one*, being dealt with accordingly; *much* being expected from that man to whom *much* had been given, and *little* being required

---

* Romans vii. 14—25. † Matt. x. 26. Mark iv. 22, &c.
‡ Matt. xxv. 31—40.

from him to whom had been committed *little*. Our
Saviour spoke also distinctly about REWARDS and
PUNISHMENTS. He told His disciples, clearly and
repeatedly, that the *slightest* act of single-hearted
service on the part of God's children, should receive
express reward. The secret prayer, silent alms-deed,
the unobtrusive act of fasting, the cup of cold water
given to a disciple, should be returned in an abundant
recompense.* Moreover, he by whom the hungry
should be fed, the naked clothed, the sick or the
imprisoned visited, the stranger lodged, should find
his deeds recorded with the spirit in which they had
been performed, and dealt with in exact accordance.†
Whereas, neglect of duty towards God, neglect of
the just exercise of love towards men, profession of
religion without sincerity,‡ were spoken of as matters
to be punished at the hand of the Great King and
Judge.

The language of the *Apostles* likewise was decided.
We need not quote from them passage by passage,
as all that they have said must be familiar to the
Bible reader. It might suffice to state that the
ACTS OF THE APOSTLES, the EPISTLES, and the
BOOK OF REVELATION are in perfect harmony, declaring plainly not only that God hath appointed a
day in the which He will judge the world in righteousness, by that man whom he hath ordained,"§ but
also that He will in that day "try every man's work
of what sort it is"‖ and "judge the secrets of men,"¶

* Matt. vi. 1, 18.
‡ Matt. xxv. 25—28, and 41—45.
‖ 1 Corinthians iii. 13—15.
† Matt. xii. 36.
§ Acts xvii. 31.
¶ Romans ii. 16.

so that "every one may receive the things done in his body, according to that he hath done, whether it be good or bad."* But perhaps we may not be deemed wearisome, if we pause for an instant to consider one of all these harmonizing testimonies separately: namely, that which is afforded in the *twentieth chapter* of the REVELATION. The words are few, but they draw a wondrous picture of the awful scene by which that last great act of judgment shall be marked. "And I saw a GREAT WHITE THRONE, and Him that sat on it, from whose face the earth and the heaven fled away; and there was found no place for them. And I saw the dead, small and great, stand before God; AND THE BOOKS WERE OPENED; and ANOTHER BOOK WAS OPENED, WHICH IS THE BOOK OF LIFE; and the dead were judged out of those things which were written in the books *according to their works.* And the SEA gave up the dead which were in it: and DEATH and HELL (or, the grave) delivered up the dead which were in them; and they were judged every man *according to their works.* And DEATH and HELL were cast into the LAKE OF FIRE. This is the SECOND DEATH. AND WHOSOEVER WAS NOT FOUND WRITTEN IN THE BOOK OF LIFE WAS CAST INTO THE LAKE OF FIRE." Thus far then is evident: There will be a formal opening of the "Books" wherein are entered all the good and evil men have wrought while in the body. What these "Books" are, we know not. Whether *actual Records*, with the thoughts, words, and actions of mankind, exist, to be produced at the appointed

* 2 Corinthians v. 10. Galatians vi 7 and 8

hour of Judgment, we know not, nor need we seek to know. Let it suffice that every secret shall be known, that so full justice may be done, and men, both saved and unsaved, may be judged according to their works. But now "ANOTHER BOOK" is spoken of as being opened afterwards, which is called "THE BOOK OF LIFE."—We may suppose, then, that when the judgment has been passed upon *the works* of every man, according to their actual merits or demerits, as found written in *the various books first opened*, and all the world,—those on the *right* hand and those on the *left*,—are proved guilty before God; "THE BOOK OF LIFE" will be brought forward, wherein *man's works have no place at all*. This Book, we may presume, tells only of the LOVE, POWER, GRACE, ATONEMENT, and INTERCESSION of the Lord Jesus Christ, and bears upon its pages the beloved names of those who, through the mighty power of the Eternal Spirit, have been brought to see their state of condemnation, have cried out fervently to God for mercy, and have gone with simple faith to the Redeemer, and laid all their sins on His atoning cross. Through grace *they have believed;* through grace *they have maintained their heavenly course;* and now, complete in grace, *they stand, without a fear, at the right hand of the Eternal Judge.* Nothing have they whereof they should boast: nothing by which any of them might be found worthy, so far as their own doings in the flesh have been concerned. The former Books have proved that every one of them is guilty before God. His repentance has found need to be repented of, his tears have wanted washing, and his washen tears have needed to be washed again in the blood of the Redeemer. But *by grace he is what he is*, a pardoned, justified, sanctified, and saved soul: a child of God: an heir of glorious immortality. "The Book of Life" contains his name. And now *his poor imperfect works do follow him*. Have they been wrought with singleness of heart towards God? Have they been done with a sincere desire to glorify His Word; with fervent love towards Him; and in sincere brotherhood with His Redeemed People. If so, then we must ask, *In what degree? How fervent* has been the desire? *How deep* the love? *How close* the brotherhood? for the eternal *crown* shall be accordingly. "As one star differeth from another star in glory, so also is the resurrection of the dead." Although, when the works stood *by themselves* for judgment, their actual merits being tested by the former books, they could do nothing but condemn; yet, *now that they stand forth as the efforts*, (weak indeed, and very faulty,) *of the heart renewed by the Eternal Spirit's grace*, they are accepted IN CHRIST JESUS; their sinfulness is all washed out in His atoning blood, and their sincerity, which was through grace, abides in the pure garment of the Saviour's Righteousness.

Upon those whose names shall be found written in this Book of Life, the blessings of eternal glory will abide; they shall inherit everlasting happiness:—the peace of the "NEW JERUSALEM" shall be their portion for an everlasting age. Of their estate of glory in that heavenly city we shall have to speak in our next chapter. For the present, let us be content to note, that every believer in the Lord Jesus, standing on the right hand of the Redeemer's throne, shall find his name recorded in THE LAMB'S BOOK OF LIFE; and He who shall be seated on the throne, will make confession of his name before His father and the holy angels, and will say to him, "WELL DONE, GOOD AND FAITHFUL SERVANT, ENTER THOU INTO THE JOY OF THY LORD."

But as to those whose names shall NOT be written in the BOOK OF LIFE,—it is declared that their eternal portion is "THE LAKE OF FIRE."

They did not confess the Lord while they were yet on earth, and now the Lord will not confess their names before His Father which is in Heaven. They who rejected Him must be themselves rejected. They who dishonored him must be themselves dishonored. They who set at nought His counsel and would none of His reproof, must "eat the fruit of their own ways, and be filled with their own devices." They will plead, "Lord, have we not eaten and drunk in thy presence, and hast Thou not taught in our streets? Have we not in Thy name cast out devils, and done many wonderful works?"* *But their pleading will be ALL IN VAIN.* The door of MERCY will be shut by the stern hand of JUSTICE; and the word of Christ will be, "I never knew you, depart from me all ye workers of iniquity," and, as it is elsewhere given, "Depart from me ye cursed, into everlasting fire, prepared for the devil and his angels." And they

---

* Matthew vii. 22, Luke xiii. 26.

shall go away into everlasting punishment,* in the
LAKE OF FIRE.

O that the *ungodly*, the *careless*, the *worldly*, and
all those who have *put off the matters of salvation to
a future day*, would think whether it is worth their
while to live as they are living, when at any moment
they may be called hence, and nothing but a fearful
looking-for of this tremendous sentence be their portion till that day in which they shall *receive* it. O
that they would calmly think whether it is not the
part of wisdom *to break off at once from all iniquity*,
and GIVE THEIR HEARTS TO GOD. Forgive me,
reader—"*Who can dwell with the devouring flames!*"
Who will be so great *a fool* as to allow his NEVER-
DYING SOUL to glide on smoothly towards SO TERRI-
BLE A CONDEMNATION, when the Great Lord Himself
has promised him a full and free salvation, through
HIS own priceless BLOOD AND RIGHTEOUSNESS, if he
will come from the unholy paths which worldlings
tread, and in sincerity and truth accept it at His
hands!

With this dread sentence on the wicked, it appears
that the last session of the Great Almighty Judge
will terminate. And now what further shall prevent
the Son of Man *resigning the Millennial Throne?*
He has reigned till *all his enemies* have been put
beneath his feet, and DEATH has been consigned for
ever to the lake of fire. Christ *was* to reign till all
this should be done;—as it is written,—"*Then* cometh
the end, *when* he shall have put down all rule, and
all authority and power. *For He must reign, till*

* Matthew xxv. 46.

He hath put all enemies under His feet. THE LAST
LAST ENEMY THAT SHALL BE DESTROYED IS DEATH."*
But clearly, it is as the SON OF MAN, reigning over
the children of Adam *upon the earth*, and in this
sense alone, His reign is then to terminate.   Having
as the Son of Man, put down, and thoroughly subdued all wicked principalities, authorities, and powers,
and put all enemies,—even death—under His feet;
He will, *as Son of Man*, deliver up the *earthly* kingdom, wherein these opponents of His reign existed,
into the hands of the ETERNAL FATHER.   STILL HE
WILL BE KING; still He will reign; still, exalted
high upon the Throne of Glory, He will sit and rule.
The NEW, THE HEAVENLY JERUSALEM will be the
place wherein, among the true and holy ISRAEL
redeemed from every nation of the earth, He will
delight to manifest His presence, and exalt His love.
There shall it be recorded for the everlasting age,
that THE REDEEMER LIVES and REIGNS; *there* upon
the THRONE OF DAVID, although not after any earthly
manner, He will sit "to order it and to establish it
.... for ever."   And there shall it be seen that
"OF THE INCREASE OF HIS GOVERNMENT AND PEACE,
THERE SHALL BE NO END."

And thus, although it will be true that "the Son
also Himself shall be subject unto Him that put all
things under Him, that God may be all in all;"† yet
will it be only a subjection of the MANHOOD for the
magnification of the GODHEAD.   And so the reign of
Christ will be as actual *then* and *for the everlasting
age*, as when God gave to Him "the heathen for His

---

* 1 Corinthians xv. 24—26.   † 1 Corinthians xv. 27, 28.

inheritance, and the uttermost parts of the earth for His possession."

With this resignation of the earthly kingdom into the Eternal Father's hand will the momentous Evening of the Day of Judgment close,—upon this will follow instantly, (for there will be no night except in Hell,) THE DAWN OF THE ETERNAL DAY OF GLORY. Then will be the shout, "Lift up your heads, O ye gates, and be ye lift up, ye everlasting doors, and the King of Glory shall come in." Then will be the blissful welcome from the Hosts who never fell, to the Redeemed from earth. Then will "the multitude which no man can number, out of all nations, and kindreds, and people, and tongues," stand forth before the throne, and before the Lamb, clothed with white robes and palms in their hands; and, rendering heavenly praise for their salvation, enter on a blissful service of the Lord who bought them with His blood. And glorious and supremely happy shall their portion be. No care, no cross, no fear, no sin. But blessings,— richest blessings, such as eye hath never seen, nor ear heard of, nor the heart conceived; for in their Father's House shall be their glorious abode, and in His manifested presence they shall offer praise; and "THE LAMB, WHICH IS IN THE MIDST OF THE THRONE, SHALL FEED THEM, AND SHALL LEAD THEM TO LIVING FOUNTAINS OF WATERS; AND GOD SHALL WIPE AWAY ALL TEARS FROM THEIR EYES."

14

CHAPTER IX.

THE NEW JERUSALEM.

"And I, John, saw the holy city, New Jerusalem, coming down from God out of heaven, prepared as a bride adorned for her husband."—REV. xxi. 2.

THE Heaven and the earth shall flee away, from the bright shining of His face, who will be seated on the Great White Throne of Judgment. This is a plainly stated fact, on which we need not be ashamed to decline offering comment. No thoughtful person will be disposed to blame us for receiving it *without remark*, as it is placed before us in the language of the inspired St. John,—"And I saw a Great White Throne, and Him that sat on it, from whose face the earth and the heaven fled away; and there was found no place for them."* It is enough for us, that again and again we are forewarned of this amazing fact in Holy Scripture; so that if we receive the testimony of the word of God *at all*, we cannot but look forward to a time when "Heaven and earth shall pass away." God has not told us more than the *bare fact*. Let this then be enough. But an event, both great and wonderful will *follow* upon this, concerning which we find much information, and in which we are peculiarly interested: I mean, THE NEW CREATION. "Be-

* Revelation xx. 11.

hold," said He that sat upon the throne to the beloved John—"BEHOLD, I MAKE ALL THINGS NEW."*

Let us observe, with care, now what is said concerning this.

ISAIAH, in the *sixty-fifth chapter*, in which he also speaks with plainness of the blessings of the Millennial Reign of Peace, carries us beyond it for an instant, saying by the word of the Lord—"The former troubles are forgotten, and . . . . they are hid from mine eyes. For, behold, I CREATE NEW HEAVENS, AND A NEW EARTH: and the former shall not be remembered, nor come into mind. But, be ye glad and rejoice for ever in that which I create: for, behold, I create Jerusalem a rejoicing, and her people a joy." Having thus spoken, the Prophet evidently draws back from this glorious new creation, to the *type* of it which is to be afforded by the Millennial period, in which, though curbed exceedingly, both *sin* and *death* will have *their* place.

But let us take another word of testimony. If we turn to THE FIRST EPISTLE OF ST. PETER, *the third chapter*, we shall read as follows:—"Seeing then that all these things must be dissolved, what manner of persons ought ye to be in all holy conversation and godliness; looking for, and hasting unto the coming of the Day of God, wherein the heavens being on fire shall be dissolved, and the elements shall melt with fervent heat! NEVERTHELESS WE, ACCORDING TO HIS PROMISE, LOOK FOR NEW HEAVENS AND A NEW EARTH, WHEREIN DWELLETH RIGHTEOUSNESS. Wherefore, beloved, *seeing that ye look for*

* Revelation xxi. 5.

such things, be diligent that ye may be found of Him in peace, without spot, and blameless." St. Peter has thus made it very plain, that when in the great Day of God, the heavens and the earth shall pass away, the Lord will create *new* heavens and a *new* earth, which shall be the habitation, not in any wise of those who err, and fall, and sin; but of the righteous who are saved to life eternal.

But let us turn to the most full and clear description which God has afforded us of this in all His word. We shall find it in the *twenty-first* and *twenty-second chapters* of the REVELATION. These chapters treat of the NEW HEAVENS and NEW EARTH exclusively. It will repay us if we follow closely some part of the account there given.

Beginning then with the first verse, we read, "And I saw a NEW HEAVEN and a NEW EARTH: for the first heaven and the first earth were passed away." Here we have the fulfilment *in vision,* of the prophecy which was previously uttered by the Prophets, by our Lord Himself, and by the Apostles. Now in whatever *other* particulars of a physical kind, the NEW EARTH is to differ from the earth of the Millennial period, there is *one* point which will make a very clear distinction between them. In the Millennial age—THE SEA is particularly spoken of, and frequently referred to among the blessings which will be enjoyed by Israel and the nations.* But St. John declares pointedly in the description of his vision of the NEW EARTH,—"AND THERE WAS NO MORE SEA." This matter seems to be recorded in order to prevent

* See Chapter VI.

any risk of confusion in the mind, concerning the *Millennial* and the *Post-millennial* earth. The *one* is to have *sea;* indeed the sea is to be *very* essential to the well-being of its people;—the *other* is to have *no sea.* None will be needed either for beauty or utility.

Having thus spoken, John continues, "And I saw THE HOLY CITY, NEW JERUSALEM, *coming down from God, out of Heaven*, prepared as a bride adorned for her husband. And I heard a great voice out of Heaven, saying, Behold the tabernacle of God is with men, and He will dwell with them, and they shall be His people, and God Himself shall be with them, and be their God. And God shall wipe away all tears from their eyes: and *there shall be no more death*, neither sorrow, nor crying, neither shall there be any more pain; for the former things are passed away. And He that sat upon the Throne said, BEHOLD, I MAKE ALL THINGS NEW. And He said unto me, Write; for these words are true and faithful."

We observe here, that there is no mention of a city to be *built* upon the earth, as in the vision of EZEKIEL. The NEW JERUSALEM is *not to be built*, but it is *to come down out of Heaven* from God. To *come down* to earth, and thereupon abide, its foundations being fixed by God in their appointed place. Earth made pure by fire, and formed anew, will be prepared by God for all "the nations of them which are saved," and New Jerusalem will be its wonderful METROPOLIS, the CENTRE of its LIGHT, and LIFE, and GLORY.

But let us turn our thoughts now more particularly, —as we follow the Apostle's vision,—to the *construc-*

tion, *dimensions*, and *character* of this NEW JERU-
SALEM.

As we pass down the chapter upon which we have
been commenting, and also that which follows it, we
find it recorded that the city is to have "THE GLORY
OF GOD," her light being "like unto a stone most precious, even like a jasper stone, clear as crystal."
Thus we surely learn that the glory of the saints'
eternal city will be great indeed. So great, that it
is recorded, the city shall have "no need of the sun,
neither of the moon, to shine in it," because of the
superior brightness of the glory of the Lord. Moreover, by reason of this glory, *day* and *night* will not
be recognized. The light which is "above the brightness of the sun" will shine unceasingly; wherefore
"there shall be no night there: and they shall need
no candle, neither light of the sun; for the Lord God
shall give them light."*

But again: The city is to have "A WALL, great and
high;" "TWELVE GATES," guarded by angels of the
Lord, and having "the names of the twelve tribes of
the Children of Israel" written upon them. Three of
these gates are to face the east,—three the north,—
three the south,—and three the west; and each of
them is to be a pearl. The wall of the city is, moreover, to have "twelve foundations, and in these
foundations are to be placed the names of the twelve .
Apostles of the Lamb." These twelve foundations
are to be garnished with all manner of precious

* We should be careful to remark that it is not said—the sun
shall never shine upon it,—but only that by reason of the brighter
glory of the Lord, the light of the Sun will not be needed.

stones. The first, jasper; the second, sapphire; the third, chalcedony; the fourth, emerald; the fifth, sardonyx; the sixth, sardius; the seventh, chrysolite; the eighth, beryl; the ninth, topaz; the tenth, chrysoprasus; the eleventh, jacinth; the twelfth, amethyst. So, indeed the God of Truth has said, to whom the riches of all worlds belong. So, doubtless, therefore, will the everlasting foundations of the new and Heavenly Jerusalem be adorned. The STREET, or rather, the "place" ($\dot{\eta}$ $\pi\lambda\alpha\tau\epsilon\iota\alpha$) of the city is also mentioned. It is to be constructed of "pure gold, as it were transparent glass."

OF SUCH EXCELLENCE AND BEAUTY, O BELIEVER IN THE SON OF GOD, IS THE GREAT CITY OF THINE EVERLASTING HOME. Rejoice then in the prospect, and cast not one wishful look upon the world behind thee. Let "ONWARD, UPWARD, HEAVENWARD, HOMEWARD, LOOKING UNTO JESUS," be thy daily motto; for the GREAT KING hath purchased with His blood, for thy saved soul, A GLORIOUS INTEREST IN THIS BRIGHT JERUSALEM.

But let us observe; there is to be NO TEMPLE in this city. In the *Millennial* Jerusalem, described so minutely by EZEKIEL, there was *a vast* Temple, as we have already seen.* But in this NEW JERUSALEM it is *not to be so.* St. John says, "And I saw no Temple therein; for the Lord God Almighty and the Lamb are the Temple of it." But there is to be that which is *far better* than a *Temple;*—even "THE THRONE OF GOD AND OF THE LAMB;" and that which is far better than the most hallowed of all *Temple worship;* for it

* See Chapter V.

is written that God's servants shall serve Him; and they shall see His face; and His name shall be written in their foreheads."

But of what dimensions shall this city be, which is, as it appears, to be the great METROPOLIS of the NEW EARTH? The measurement is given us as follows:— "The City lieth four-square, and *the length is as large as the breadth;* and he (a man with a measuring reed in his hand) measured the City with his reed, TWELVE THOUSAND FURLONGS. The length, and the breadth, and the height of it are equal." Now this at once shows that the dimensions of the City will be *enormous.* Twelve thousand furlongs, are equal to ONE THOUSAND FIVE HUNDRED MILES. The City then (having each of its sides, one thousand five hundred miles in length) would contain an area of no less than TWO MILLIONS, TWO HUNDRED AND FIFTY THOUSAND SQUARE MILES. Its height also,—inclusive of course of its *foundations,* and, perhaps also, of *internal terraces* rising one above another towards the centre,—is to be ONE THOUSAND FIVE HUNDRED MILES. But the Jasper Wall surrounding the City is to be in height "an hundred and forty and four cubits." That is to say, (taking eighteen inches to the cubit) TWO HUNDRED AND SIXTEEN FEET, —the foundations, we may suppose, not being included. Now it is implied in the most decided manner, that the NEW JERUSALEM will descend from Heaven to Earth and there be fixed for ever, as Earth's wonderful METROPOLIS.

For this we have but to look *still* at the *twenty-first chapter* of REVELATION, to which we have been principally referring in this chapter, and we shall find that when St. John had said of the new Jerusalem, that "the Glory of God did lighten it, and the Lamb is the light thereof," he added, and the *nations* of them which are saved, shall walk in the light of it: and the *kings of the earth* do bring their glory and honor into it. And the gates of it shall not be shut at all by day: for there shall be no night there. And they shall bring *the glory and honor of the nations* into it."

But should it be so, then we must suppose that when the world is re-constructed, as it were:—when it is made "A NEW EARTH;"—*its dimensions will be such as to warrant the existence of so extensive a* ME-. TROPOLIS. And where shall an objection to such a change arise? Cannot He who first formed all things out of nothing, by His word of power *enlarge* a world which He of old *called forth*, if an enlargement should be needed? Most certainly this cannot be a thing *too hard* for the Almighty.

Then *thus* we may suppose it *will* be. And on the NEW EARTH, of which the shining capital will be the NEW JERUSALEM, the saved people of the *former* earth will live and glorify the Lord their God, for ever and for ever. The Lord will have his Throne amongst them, "and they shall see His face, and His name shall be in their foreheads ...... and they shall reign for ever and ever." And from the throne of God and of the Lamb, a pure RIVER OF WATER OF LIFE shall flow,* and "in the midst of the street of it, and on either side of the river," will be found "THE TREE OF LIFE," bearing "twelve manner

* Rev. xxii. 1.

of fruits," and yielding her fruit "every month:" and the leaves of the tree will be for the service (εἰς θεραπειαν) of the nations. And there shall be no more curse."

Now what was Eden's beauty,—what Eden's excellence,—compared with that which shall be, when, in the eyes of the adoring "multitude, no man can number," the brightness of the new Jerusalem shall be revealed! Truly "eye hath not seen, nor ear heard, neither have entered into the heart of man, the things which God hath prepared for them that love Him." O reader, have you laid up your treasure in this new Jerusalem? "Blessed are they that do His commandments, that they may have right to the tree of life, and may enter in through the gates into the City."

We have, I think, seen clearly that the City described so minutely by EZEKIEL, upon the construction and situation of which we dwelt at some length in a former chapter, cannot possibly be the New Jerusalem described in the Apocalypse. The points of difference are as marked as those, on which we commented, between the *Millennial* and the *new* Earth. Amongst the more prominent, we cannot fail to have observed the following. The JERUSALEM OF EZEKIEL is to be about *nine miles* in length, and nine in breadth; covering an area of about *eighty-one square miles.* But the NEW JERUSALEM is to measure *twelve thousand furlongs,* or *one thousand five hundred miles* in length, and the same in breadth; covering an area of *two millions, two hundred and fifty thousand square miles.* Again; THE JERUSALEM OF EZEKIEL is to have a vast *Temple* within its walls wherein the service of the Lord is to be carried on continually. But THE NEW JERUSALEM is to have *no Temple whatever*, but "the Lord God Almighty and the Lamb, are" to be "the Temple of it." Again; THE JERUSALEM OF EZEKIEL is to be refreshed by a *stream of water issuing forth from under the threshold of the house* eastward, and flowing into the straits which will unite the Dead Sea with the Mediterranean,* and upon the banks of these straits "shall grow all trees for meat, whose leaf shall not fade, neither shall the fruit thereof be consumed; it shall bring forth new fruit according to his months, because their waters they issued out of the sanctuary; and the fruit thereof shall be for meat, and the leaf thereof for medicine (bruises and sores.") But THE NEW JERUSALEM is to be adorned with "*a pure river of water of life*, clear as crystal, *proceeding out of the throne of God and of the Lamb*. In the midst of the street of it, and on either side of the river," is to be "*the tree of life*," bearing "twelve manner of fruits," and yielding "her fruit every month," and the leaves of the tree are to be for the service (εἰς θεραπειαν) of the nations." And once again; the *materials* of THE JERUSALEM OF EZEKIEL are to be, for anything that appears to the contrary, of *ordinary* although *excellent* kind. But THE NEW JERUSALEM is to be built of *gold* and *precious stones*, with *gates of pearl.*

We cannot, then, confound these cities with each other. They are perfectly distinct. The one is to be *earthly*, the other *heavenly*. The one is for *time*,

* See Chapter VI.

the other for *eternity*.   Yet we cannot fail to observe
points of similarity, sufficient both in number and
strength to lead us to conclude that in the Millennial
Jerusalem of Ezekiel we have a *type* of that which
shall come down from God out of Heaven.

But now we must glance at one or two assertions
which direct our thoughts towards THE NEW EARTH
generally:—that earth of which the Heavenly City is
to be the capital.

The earth is to be gloriously peopled with "THE
NATIONS OF THEM WHICH ARE SAVED." Righteousness and glory will reign everywhere.   The glory of
God and of the Lamb, which is to be the brightness
of the New Jerusalem, will illuminate also the re-
motest regions, so that their inhabitants will "walk
in the light of it."   Surely it will not be said to contradict the received view concerning the eternal state,
if we thus suppose that *nations*, with their *kings and
divers orders of authorities and powers* will then
exist.   It *may*.—But certainly the Bible leads us to
believe that *it will be so*, nevertheless.   "The *nations*
of them which are saved," and "*the kings of the earth*,"
are spoken of in plainest terms, as being coëxistent
with the NEW JERUSALEM, and as bringing their
glory and honor into it.*   Indeed, to think it will be
otherwise, would be to think that the order of things
in the New Earth will be different from that which
has (so far as the Inspired word teaches us) existed
in any part of the Lord's kingdom, and to contradict
all analogy.   How frequently we read about "the
principalities and powers in heavenly places," the

* Revelation xxi. 24—26.

"thrones" also, and "dominions," archangels, crowned elders, angels, cherubim and seraphim. There is evidently a diversity of order and power among those who have their part already in the realms of glory. *There* are the great ones bearing rule, and *there* are those who bow beneath their sway. Nor can this orderly arrangement in a kingdom where no sin exists, disturb the happiness of any, but the opposite; it needs must minister to the increased happiness of all. For ourselves, shall we *complain*, if on the throne of that celestial nation in which our everlasting dwelling may be fixed, the Crown of Government be borne by Paul or Peter, James or John? Nay, shall we not *rejoice* exceedingly concerning this, and yield them gladly the obedience which is due? And what if Mark, or Timothy, or Barnabas, or Silas, occupy the seat of honor *next* in rank or authority,—shall we oppose our voice? Or shall we think that there would be unreasonable dealing on the part of God towards us? Nay, do we not *ourselves*, as taught by our Redeeming Lord, look forward to possess authority? If we have wrought for Him with long and earnest service, using well the talents which the Lord has given us, do we not expect accordingly, to have dominion over *ten*, or *five*, or *two* cities, as the case may be.

It is remarkable that so many people should be strongly impressed with the idea, that in "THE WORLD TO COME" all things will be *ethereal:* that our future resting-place will rather be *a space* wherein our happy spirits may fly here and there in glory, than a true *substantial world*, where men in actual bodies may abide and carry on such works as shall be found consistent with their glorified estate.

Now, it is certain from the Word of God that every redeemed soul is to be clothed, before he enters on his heavenly glory, with *a body;* a substantial body; a body like that of our Lord in which He rose again; a body having flesh and bones.* That is to say, the very body which was dead and buried, is to be again assumed, but rendered *incorruptible,* and meet for Heaven.

Our Saviour's resurrection was the type of ours. *As* He rose, *so* shall we rise. Thus St. Paul teaches us, in the *fifteenth chapter* of the *first Epistle to the* Corinthians,—"Now is Christ risen from the dead, and become the first fruits of them that slept. . . . . Every man in his own order: Christ the first-fruits, afterwards they that are Christ's at His coming." But if so, then we need not try to explain away the clear assertions of the Scripture as to the *substantial nature* of the New Jerusalem. The fact that there shall be Nations with their Kings,—that there shall be Christ's table, at which the Redeemed shall eat and drink with Him,—that there shall be water of life and trees of life—of which the nations of God's saved people may partake,—presents for our acceptance no peculiar difficulty. Do we not call to mind how Jesus, being raised again, took bread and fish and an honeycomb and did eat before His won-

---

* No mention has been made of *blood.* Indeed, it is probable that our Saviour's risen body had no blood. It is written "flesh and *blood* cannot inherit the kingdom of God." The presence of blood implies that which is corruptible.—1 Cor. xv. 50.

dering disciples? How He entered into the house
with two of them, and sat there as beforetime, and,
took bread, and blessed it, and brake, and gave to
them? Surely He was the self-same Jesus. His
hands, and feet, and side, were witnesses of this.
And, except only when their eyes were holden, His
disciples *knew Him.* But *in this very body*, He now
sits enthroned above. The "flesh and bones" with
which the Lord ascended, are not found unworthy of
the Father's glory, nor inconsistent with the residence of *spiritual* beings of the *highest* and the *holiest*
ranks. There is no objection, then, to things *sub-*
stantial even in the Heaven of Heavens!

What room then can we find for hesitation? We
are to be actually MEN. As truly so as we are now.
Not spirits, for "a spirit hath not flesh and bones."
And why may not the EARTH, renewed, regenerated,
made free from the pollutions of iniquity, by God's
all-purging fires, and formed again of such dimensions
as are needful for the *multitudes* of the Redeemed,—
be our eternal place of rest and glory? Why *must*
we dwell on the idea that some far distant *star* or
space above, is to receive us when the Trumpet of
the Lord shall sound for resurrection? True,—we
are to *meet* Christ *"in the air"* at first, and perhaps
to enter with Him through the pearly gates of NEW
JERUSALEM, and join His people at the marriage
supper, while the City is suspended in the heights
above. *But this will not be for eternity.* When
JERUSALEM descends upon the new-created EARTH, it
would appear that we are likewise to descend, and
earth adorned in new-born beauty will be our abode.

No roaring sea, no storms, no pestilence, no war, no misery, no sin, no Satan, no unholy flesh, are to disturb; but it will be EARTH no less, and men in actual bodies will inhabit it. What powers will be possessed by our renewed bodies we are not informed. "It doth not yet appear what we shall be. But we know that . . . . . . we shall be like" Christ.* We know that we shall "shine forth as the sun in the kingdom of our Father."† We know that we shall be in everlasting joy and glory.‡ What matter then is it to us for *speculation*, what shall be our powers of body or of mind? The day will soon reveal itself, and we shall know as we are known.

But concerning *our position* in the NEW EARTH, there are one or two *important* questions (so at least they seem to be to some) which we must now consider.

SHALL WE KNOW AGAIN THE FRIENDS WHOM WE HAVE LOVED IN THIS, OUR LIFE OF SIN, AND LOVE THEM STILL WITH CLOSE ATTACHMENT AS OF OLD? I will not hesitate a moment to reply—"UNDOUBTEDLY WE SHALL."—*As* the disciples, (except only when *their eyes* were holden) knew their risen Lord: *as* Abraham knew and spoke of Lazarus: *as* many from the East and West are to sit down with Abraham, and Isaac, and Jacob, in the Kingdom of Heaven: *so* shall be the recognition. What did Paul mean but to declare this doctrine, when he said "I would not have you to be ignorant, brethren, *concerning*

---

* 1 John iii. 2.   † Matthew xiii. 43.

‡ Matthew xxv. 21, 23, 34, 46; John xvii. 22, 24; 1 Peter i. 3, 5; Revelation vii. 13—17, &c., &c.

them which are asleep, that ye sorrow not, even as others which have no hope. For if we believe that Jesus died and rose again, even so them also which sleep in Jesus will God bring with him . . . . . . The dead in Christ shall rise first: then we which are alive and remain, shall be caught up *together with them* in the clouds . . . wherefore *comfort one another* with these words!* Or when, again, the same apostle said, "What is our hope, or joy, or crown of rejoicing? Are not even *ye*, in the presence of our Lord Jesus Christ, at His coming?† What had he in mind, unless it was the firm impression that in Heaven there would be a recognition amongst those who knew each other upon earth, and a continuance of that love which had united them so closely in their state of trial! No doubt there will be recognition. No doubt the people of the Lord will carry on and perfect that attachment which on earth was found so sweet and so encouraging.

But then, the question *will* arise, "*O what about those dear ones who will not be found in Heaven?* Those many *parents, husbands, wives, children;* loved,—yes *deeply* loved,—but lost,—because they would not have the Lord's salvation? Will it not be a fearful flaw in our eternal happiness—will it not for ever mar our glorious peace—to know that they are for eternity consigned to the unceasing flame of torment? *Will* it not? *Must* it not? It neither *must* nor *will.* THE MIND OF CHRIST in that great day of *perfect righteousness*, will be THE MIND OF EVERY SAVED SOUL. The *feelings* of the regenerated

---

* 1 Thess. iv. 13—18.   † 1 Thess. ii. 19—20.

flesh, will not (like those of the unholy flesh which clothed the spirit formerly) resist the will and work of God. There will be then no law in the members warring against the law of the mind. The will, the love, the justice of the Lord, will be in absolute accordance with the desires of every inhabitant of the NEW HEAVEN and the NEW EARTH. What God shall have decreed, in that will every soul find pleasure. *No momentary wish* will be found passing through the heart of *the least Saint* in bliss, to alter what the Lord may have appointed, or to change the state of any soul, except in full agreement with His perfect will. The various decrees, therefore, of the day of Judgment, fixing as they will have done, the everlasting destiny of every child of man, according to his works, will be precious in the sight of the Re-deemed. And though they had, in times gone by, known *fathers, mothers, husbands, wives, children,* and others, *after the flesh* (the flesh of *those* days, which could love without regard to the Lord's holy will) yet now they will know them no more. Nor will they *wish* to know them. The decree of the Almighty will have been passed concerning them, and it will be enough. The Saved will have *no mind* to serve, except THE MIND OF CHRIST, which then will reign both in their inner man and all the members of their glorious body. It may be that in *this* estate, in which the flesh is charged with the affec-tions which are natural thereto, and which endear the parent and the child, the husband and the wife, and often friend to friend, it is peculiarly difficult to com-prehend how perfect happiness can exist where the

very closest ties are to be broken, and that for ever.
But we must remember, that THE GREAT GOD who
is the GOD OF JUSTICE, but whose NAME IS LOVE,
has *power* and *goodness* which will prove *sufficient in
this thing*, as in every other. He will make *our
heavenly minds* to be in such entire conformity with
His mind, that we shall find no cause for anything:
but PRAISE by reason of *the most tremendous sentence*
which His perfect justice will see fit to execute.
Will not also the same conformity of mind, make
every saint in bliss, (the very *lowest*, just as truly
as the *highest*,) satisfied most perfectly with the
particular place which, in accordance with the just
decrees of the great day of Christ, he will be called
to occupy?

I think, then, that the question which so frequently
arises as to the unhappiness consequent upon the
separation at the Great Day of Judgment, of so
many who have dearly loved each other upon earth,
and their consequent departure one from the other
for eternity,—has only weight, by reason of our
want of due consideration of the *natural desires*
which will be implanted in that mind which is to
be conformed entirely to THE MIND OF GOD.

But now why should any one allow a doubt to rise
within him upon any point concerning the true peace
of the believer when he shall enter the eternal glory?
Has not the Lord Jesus spoken plainly. Have not
the Apostles and the Prophets borne their witness in
the word of an unerring inspiration—Is it not clear
by the unwavering testimony of God's Book of Truth
—THAT THE RIGHTEOUS SHALL INHERIT EVERLAST-

ING HAPPINESS—THE JOY OF THEIR LORD—A PEACE, A REST, A STATE OF SATISFACTION IN WHICH NOT A FAULT SHALL BE DISCERNED, NOR ANY WANT BE KNOWN? Is it not said that "the Lamb which is in the midst of the Throne shall feed them, and shall lead them unto living fountains of waters; and GOD SHALL WIPE AWAY ALL TEARS FROM THEIR EYES"? And shall we, in the face of all this testimony, think that there will be *aught of misery* in our blissful future? O NO: *let us bid the thought for ever cease.* IT CANNOT BE. We have no choice but to look forward with rejoicing confidence to that estate of bliss which the NEW HEAVEN and NEW EARTH will presently reveal.

Now for this glorious inheritance let *us*—my readers —stand prepared. The blood-washed vestment, the over-wrapping robe of the Redeemer's Righteousness, —in these we must be clothed. By faith, which is through grace, we must array ourselves. And with our burning lamp of spiritual life, and the well sharpened sword of the Eternal Spirit, in the continual grasp of hands, made strong by persevering prayer, we must await the Saviour's coming; so that when He shall appear to call His people hence, we may not be ashamed, but enter into the very chamber of His presence, and, in His good time, take our appointed lot in the Eternal World, where dwelleth righteousness, and peace, and joy, and glory, before Him who sitteth on the Throne, and before the Lamb; that we may serve and magnify our Great and Glorious God forever and forever.

So then have we introduced our readers,—following, as we trust, the simple teaching of the Bible,—through the eventful EVENTIDE of our poor fallen earth, to the bright dawn of the most glorious Day of EARTH'S REGENERATION. And here we find ourselves at the *last* point of information given in the Word of God. THE DAY, THE EVERLASTING DAY OF RIGHTEOUSNESS AND GLORY, is opened to our view, and the Inspired Volume closes.

And what need we more? LET US BUT PRESS ONWARD, CLOTHED WITH CHRIST, AND HAVING CHRIST ABIDING IN OUR HEARTS; and those most precious things, of which no doubt it is not possible for man in this poor fallen state to speak, will be opened to our view, and by experience we shall learn their excellence, and before GOD REJOICE WITH JOY WHICH IS UNSPEAKABLE AND FULL OF GLORY.

CHAPTER X.

CONCLUSION.

"Wherefore, beloved. seeing that ye look for such things, be diligent that ye may be found of Him in peace, without spot and
blameless."—2 PETER iii. 14.

WE have been dealing, in these chapters, with the
deep things of the Divine Word. But sincerely do I
trust that they have not been handled with presumption. We have endeavored to face every difficulty
but in a meek and prayerful spirit. Occasion has
arisen frequently to refer to the *prophetic periods;*
but it will not be said that we have spoken with unseemly positiveness about the veiled future, as to
days, and months, and years. Those periods which
have been sealed already by the pages of *past* history
have been spoken of with some degree of positiveness:
but no others have been referred to, except, it may
have been to strengthen watchfulness by offering an
extra point of *probability.*

Very much, however, which has been advanced in
the foregoing pages, may have appeared *strange* to
those who have been used to entertain with strictness
the more ordinary views concerning the prophetic
writings. If what has been advanced has not convinced these persons,—we would only say,—Let us
not be too severe one towards another, because we see

things in a different light; but rather let us *pray for one another*, and for the whole Church of Christ, that God may grant each member thereof, the spirit of a right discernment. *If God's children disputed less, and prayed more, it would be far better.* There would be more light, more wisdom, more faith, more love, more peace, more holiness.

The object of these chapters has been tô excite, if possible, amongst our fellow-believers, *a more earnest and diligent study of the Scriptures, and a more constant watchfulness and unwavering preparedness for the Coming of our Lord.* There has been no endeavor to arouse an undue curiosity, nor to satisfy the minds of those who love to speculate upon "the times and the seasons, which the Father hath put in His own power." If, then, our God will make this little work a means of comfort, or of strength to any of its readers; or if He will bless it with His Spirit, that it may be the instrument of awakening any one poor unsaved soul, the object will be gained.

We have considered EIGHT of the most important subjects which the Bible has presented to the consideration of the Christian. Many things connected with these subjects have an intimate concern both with the *present* and the *past*, but all of them bear strongly upon the *future*, and with urgency exhort each one of us—"PREPARE TO MEET THY GOD."

As we have considered the several points of moment one by one, we cannot fail, I think, to have discerned the fact that we must be approaching very near to the Great Day when Christ shall call His people hence. *How* near, we have not presumed to ask. But *near, very* near, *so* near that the *waiting, watching,* attitude, is that which comes before us as the only safe position for a man on earth. AT ANY MOMENT, (if what we have gathered from the Word of God is to be rested on,) THE GREAT ARCHANGEL'S VOICE MAY SOUND, FOR ALL THE DEAD IN CHRIST TO RISE, AND ALL THE RIGHTEOUS LIVING TO BE CHANGED. For *what remains yet unaccomplished?* Surely, *if* it be true that the everlasting Gospel has been preached to every nation, *for a witness: if* the eighth Headship of the Roman Empire—"the Beast that was, and is not, and yet is"—be seated on the throne: *if* many be running to and fro, and knowledge be increasing: *if* the children of Judah be prepared to take a fresh possession of their promised land, and the land be even now in readiness for such possession, and there need nothing but a hand of power and will, to lead them back:—then *certainly* THE TIME IS SHORT; wherefore there is necessity to stand at once and constantly upon the watch-tower; and there is a loud and urgent call for prayer, for clothing with God's panoply, and for firm and constant walking in the love of Christ.

Nay, more,—for even now, THE EVILS OF THE LAST DAYS give us warning of their quick approach, and lift their voice on high, that every one who values his immortal soul, and is concerned about the glory of the Lord, should put his armor on, and stand forth ready for the fight.

What means this INFIDELITY sitting in high places, calling itself *Christ's religion,* and gaining hearing with the educated people of the world: exercising marvellous control over the minds of those towards whom we look as future pastors of our churches, and educators of our youth? What means the no less evil and increasing sway of so-called SPIRITUALISM, which puts forth its creed, and undermines in the most subtle way the truths of Holy Writ? What means that "broad" unholy doctrine which gives one hand to the Roman harlot, and the other to the false prophet of the East, and proclaims Heaven to be the resting place of the *sincere* disciples of them both, and of all people, so that they be only *earnest*, of whatever sects besides? What means that spirit which professes to hold fast by the inspired Word, and speaks of *Christ* but *no Atonement, Heaven* but *no Hell?*

These and other heresies abound on every side. They do their work where least we should expect it. They are very mighty instruments of Satan, making many sad whom God has not made sad, and causing many to fall greviously, who did run well. Thus in our own day, at home and abroad, is many a wretched wall built up, and daubed with untempered mortar; thus are pillows sewn to *all* arm-holes; thus are kerchiefs placed upon the head of *every* stature, TO HUNT SOULS withal: and the cry is "*peace, peace,* where there is *no peace.*"

Nor do we hear of an abatement in the PRACTICE of iniquity. There is WARFARE, cruel, bitter, prompted by a hatred which is fearful. DRUNKENNESS, which slays its thousands upon thousands, (sixty thousand, even in our own dear *Christian* nation, annually.) FORNICATION, the extent of which is terrible in every land. SABBATH-BREAKING, FRAUD, DECEIT, abounding to an extent which is most lamentable.

What can we say, then? Will God suffer that His Name and Word should be despised so greatly for any long extended period? Most surely He will not. Do but look upon our great advantages; our light; our knowledge; the education among rich and poor; the full and simple way in which the Gospel is now preached in nearly every nation under Heaven: and then observe the state of fearful sin and darkness in which such multitudes of men are living; hearing, knowing, understanding, but *resolved to sin*. Surely the time *must* be short. It must be even now an *advanced hour* in this "EARTH'S EVENTIDE."

BUT IF SO, THEN DOES AN ESPECIAL DUTY LIE UPON EVERY CHILD OF GOD, BOTH TOWARDS

"THE WORLD AND THE CHURCH,"

that he let his light shine brilliantly and with a steady flame before the *one*, and that he walk in holy fellowship with the *other*.

THE WORLD "lieth in wickedness" and "passeth away."* Let every Christian see that he behave before it as a Christian *should* behave; bearing the cross; fearless of the reproach; knowing how to speak a word in season, both in wisdom and in love.

THE CHURCH has enemies outside her pale, and within her very bosom. It is her day of *trial*. Her members, therefore, must both *pray* and *act in fellowship*. They must have a care for one another, such

* 1 John v. 19 and ii. 17.

as their close brotherhood demands; bearing in mind, always, the temptations and infirmities of *weaker* brethren, and leading them with tender, loving hands; feeding them with spiritual things, in wisdom and with prayer; taking heed that they can find no cause to note *appearances* of evil in the walk and conversation of their elders. Moreover, let that member of the Church who "thinketh he standeth, take heed lest he fall."

AGAIN; ON EVERY WAITING SERVANT OF THE LORD, THERE LIES RESPONSIBILITY OF NO INDIFFERENT KIND, RESPECTING

"ISRAEL AND ANTICHRIST."

"Pray for the peace of JERUSALEM; they shall prosper that love thee." As Israel's sons are looking towards their land, God's Gentile people must be ready to give help when help is needed. Never must they be unmindful of the debt they owe—under God—to Israel, of whom, as concerning the flesh, Christ came. For the *conversion* of "the Remnant," for the *Restoration* of the kingdom, and for the *Salvation* of "all Israel," must their constant prayer be made, and ready help afforded.

Moreover, knowing what the Jewish people are to suffer at the hand of ANTICHRIST, and remembering how all *other* nations likewise are to be bound up in their affliction, it behoves God's people everywhere, to bear "*that wicked one*" in memory before the Lord, and pray that his dread hand of persecution may be stayed, and that,—according to the promise given,—"for the elect's sake" the time of trial may "be shortened." And besides this, seeing how the multitudes of earth will be seduced by the usurper's subtlety, or driven to unjust compliances by his extended rod of persecution; it is incumbent on every servant of the Lord to keep the eye of faith fixed *singly* and *firmly* on the Redeemer, JESUS CHRIST; to hold fast by the WORD OF INSPIRATION; to allow nothing to obtain a footing in his creed, but that which is *revealed clearly* in the BIBLE; to suffer no opinions, works, or systems, put forth by any man, however high in public estimation, to interfere with a simple resting upon CHRIST, and CHRIST ALONE: no, nor even to obtain the slightest shadow of regard, unless they *accord absolutely* with the teaching of the HOLY BOOK OF GOD. "PROVE ALL THINGS; HOLD FAST THAT WHICH IS GOOD." "PROVE," by the *Bible;* "HOLD FAST," with *Prayer.*

AGAIN; THE SHORTNESS OF OUR TIME CALLS LOUDLY UPON EVERY MAN AND BIDS HIM BEAR IN MIND THAT WHEN THE ANTICHRIST SHALL HAVE FULFILLED HIS DAY,

"THE ADVENT"

OF THE SON OF MAN WILL BE REVEALED. To this, the mind of every earnest Christian is directed, for he knows that it will be his introduction into everlasting rest.

ARE YOU, DEAR READER, LOOKING FOR THE ADVENT? O remember what an awful matter it will be, when "one shall be taken and the other left," to be among the multitude who shall be "*left*"!

But we will not suppose that there is any doubt concerning this. You are, we will believe, in truth, like every faithful servant, waiting for your Lord's appearing. Yet we must not be unmindful of the Adversary's subtlety, nor of the sad weakness of the mortal flesh. Therefore it will not be wrong to urge on you,—"*Be diligent* that you may be found of Him in peace, without spot and blameless." Beware therefore, of lukewarmness. Shun all promptings to a carnal or a worldly spirit. Be decided, bold, determined; and yet humble, meek, and prayerful. Think not that *the foot of the cross* is a place too low for the decided Christian. Humble yourself often there. *From thence* look up; look where you will; even to the right hand of God, and see a seat upon the Saviour's throne prepared for you to occupy at the Lord's glorious Advent. The Cross! How blest a station truly! In that cross, is concentrated the great ALL IN ALL of the immortal soul's salvation.

But again; A little while and the Good Lord will interfere on the behalf of Israel, oppressed beneath the iron rule of Antichrist, and with His saints descend to earth for the first act of the Great Judgment Day,

"THE JUDGMENT OF THE NATIONS."

For this, He will descend in glory "with His Saints." Let Christians note this well,—They who shall have been caught up to meet the Saviour Jesus in the air, will come again with Him, when He descends to "judge the nations righteously" and introduce His reign. But if it will be so, and if this great foretold event be almost at the doors,—"what manner of persons ought we to be in all holy conversation and godliness!" Is it that we are to form a part of the Almighty's awful train, when "every eye shall see Him . . . . and all the kindred of the earth shall wail because of Him?" Then let us examine ourselves closely, by the standard of the *Word* and *Life* of CHRIST, and seek His grace to live. more absolutely to His glory.

And again, when this first act of the Lord's Judgment shall be numbered with the great events passed by, and

"THE REIGN OF RIGHTEOUSNESS AND PEACE"

shall have been introduced, how happy for this fallen world! But let us think, how far more blissful will be the Estate of those who living in this world are really Christ's! They will have entered on the morning of that glorious "FOR EVER WITH THE LORD;" that wonderful abiding in the presence of the King of Kings; that indissoluble union of the happy ones who sought salvation through His blood and righteousness; which is to be our portion when the Lord shall reign. Then we shall know the fulness of that 'word which has encouraged us so often while on earth,—"*If we suffer we shall also reign with Him.*"* But let us for an instant glance around us. Who is there among the sons of men, with such a glorious period in prospect, that will not "give all diligence to make his calling and election sure"? Alas! alas!—*How few* are those who seem to care at all about the matter! By nature man is but a poor helpless captive of the Devil's will; enchained, enslaved,—aye, "dead in trespasses and sins."† He

---

* 2 Timothy ii. 12.   † Ephesians ii. 1.

heeds not the vast blessings of the glorious future. The things which God has laid in store for all the children of His love, his eye has never seen, nor his ear heard, nor his heart conceived. They are revealed by the Eternal Spirit, and that Spirit no man has *by nature.* To him, therefore, they are but foolishness, and so, he heeds them not. Then it behoves *us,* my brethren, and sisters in Christ,—that we be earnest in our prayers for such; for if this be the state of all the careless world around us, nothing, which we know of, but THE SPIRIT OF THE LORD can rouse them, and break off their bonds. *"Pray without ceasing"** therefore, is the right injunction; and we must add thereto as a commandment no less necessary, *"Let your speech be always with grace seasoned with salt."*†

But again; Beyond the happy period of the Saviour's Reign we look, and see the great Deceiver, Satan, loosed from prison, and

"THE FINAL OUTBREAK OF EVIL" ensue speedily. But we look forward to this last grand effort of iniquity with no feelings of alarm on the behalf of any. Instant and glorious will be the shout which will echo through "the camp of the saints" and through "the Holy City,"—the shout of triumph and of praise. For in a moment will the Power of God arise, and before one of the true servants of Immanuel can be hurt by the assaulting foe, the hosts of Gog and Magog will be overthrown by fire from Heaven. We, if we are Christ's, shall see the work, and join in the grand shout of praise; our

* 1 Thess. v. 17.   † Colossians iv. 6.

shout shall be the signal for a momentary pause, and
then the DAY-BREAK, the commencement of earth's
sinless state, and the entire removal of iniquity from
the sight of man.

But let us learn a lesson here. We find "*a thousand years" of punishment* are not sufficient to subdue
the thirst of Satan after human souls. Then how
can any child of man, while yet on earth, expect to
remain free at any time from his assaults? What
need we have to watch and pray against his power
and subtlety! What need to seek sufficient strength
from God, wherewith to meet and faithfully resist
him! Remember DAVID, HEZEKIAH, PETER, these
strong men were *overthrown.* Now "*If any man lack
wisdom, let him ask of God, who giveth to all men
liberally and upbraideth not, and it shall be given
him*"*—God will "*give His Holy Spirit to them that
ask Him.*"† "*As thy day, so shall thy strength be.*"‡

And again; When all the voice of wickedness is
hushed in death, by reason of the fire of God, and
when the archangel's blast has sounded through the
earth and sea, and

"THE GENERAL RESURRECTION OF THE WICKED"

has ensued, and all the righteous *living* also, whether
in the Heavens or on Earth, are summoned to the
GREAT WHITE THRONE of JUDGMENT; not a fear will
cloud the brow of any babe in Christ. The feeblest
saint who ever bent the knee in prayer, the most
hesitating of believers, will glory in a perfect confidence; for there will be no *mingling of sheep and*

* James i. 5.   † Luke xi. 11—13.   ‡ Deut. xxxiii. 25.

goats before that awful Throne of Majesty. The King shall place "the *sheep* on His *right* hand, and the *goats* on the *left*." Then let the trembling, doubting, but still *praying* one, take courage. *Is he a believer?* Then he shall be on the *right hand* of the Throne, and SAFE beneath the smile of the Eternal Judge. His doubts and fears distress his spirit in these earthly days, but interfere in no wise with his safety. He feels his utter helplessness, he mourns over the weakness of his faith, he views with horror all the inconsistent actions of his Christian life, and goes on in a chastened spirit through life's pilgrimage. But here is a great secret which *might* give him comfort,—"NEVERTHELESS, THE FOUNDATION OF GOD STANDETH SURE." The shipwrecked sailor may be weak and helpless; but if, by some kindly hand of strength, he has been landed on a rock, his weakness is of very slight account: the rock is *firm* and *high enough* above the waves, therefore he need fear no evil. THE ROCK IS SAFE. But if so, HE *too* is secure. Let him but keep his footing there, and all must be well. The storm will surely pass ere long, and friendly hands will bear him home.

But once again. THE NEW HEAVENS and NEW EARTH are formed; and the most glorious city,

"NEW JERUSALEM,"

the centre of the New Earth's peace, descends from God. Here shall the believer rest and commune with his Lord, and with the holy angels who have known no sin; and he shall weep no more. O READER, CAN YOU SAY THIS HEAVENLY HOME IS YOURS? Can you *feel your footing* on the ROCK

16

OF AGES?" and are you abiding thereupon while all the storms of sin and care are passing over? Thence shall you be borne to this Eternal Home. O happy they who find their rest upon this ROCK! What peace they have! How sweet, though faint, a foretaste of that bliss to be revealed in New Jerusalem! O that all men who call themselves "Believers" did in truth possess it! But, alas! how can they have it, when they seek for it in such vain places and in such unseemly manner. See how they look for peace in their *religious systems, churches, sacraments, services, charities.* See how they seek for it, *arrayed in their own righteousness;* or trusting to God's *Mercy,* altogether heedless of His *Justice;* or comparing their own excellence with that of others, and so *claiming peace, as if of right.* Alas! for them. There is *no peace* for any such. They are but "like the troubled sea, when it cannot rest, whose waters cast up mire and dirt." "The way of peace they have not known." Peace is laid up IN CHRIST. In Jesus Christ the only Saviour, crucified and risen, there is peace indeed. He is "the Way, the Truth, and the Life." With faith beholding Him,—the substitute for us poor helpless sinners, bearing our iniquities, carrying our sorrows; washing out our guilt, which had been laid on Him, in His most precious blood, and making full atonement, that the Divine Justice of the Triune God might be entirely satisfied,—we hear the wonderful command come forth from the Eternal Throne of the ALL-HOLY ONE, with power to reach the case of every sinner upon earth, "BELIEVE ON THE LORD JESUS

CHRIST, AND THOU SHALT BE SAVED."
With faith beholding Jesus *thus*, we have true peace
indeed; a peace which passeth understanding; yea,
we have a "*joy* unspeakable and full of glory."

In NEW JERUSALEM at the bright dawning of THE
EVERLASTING DAY, which shall succeed the EVENTIDE
through which our Earth must pass, do I sincerely
pray that God may grant that those into whose hands
this book may fall, will find their GLORIOUS INHERIT-
ANCE, and in its glad possession, sing the praises of
the Lamb in "THE NEW SONG" which the Redeemed
alone can sing; and with a voice, attuned to Heaven's
harmony, unite with the "ten thousand times ten
thousand, and thousands of thousands," who shall be
gathered around the Throne of the Almighty King,
to render adoration such as angels offer, saying
"WORTHY IS THE LAMB THAT WAS SLAIN,
TO RECEIVE POWER, AND RICHES, AND
WISDOM, AND STRENGTH, AND HONOR,
AND GLORY, AND BLESSING."

APPENDIX.

THE REMOVAL OF THE CHURCH BEFORE THE APOCA-
LYPTIC JUDGMENTS—THE SEVERAL STAGES OF THE
TRANSLATION, AND CORRELATIVE THEMES.

THIS is a subject that is creating considerable interest among millennarian students, and is eliciting
much inquiry. I have often been requested to give
the scriptural proofs, that the Church (or the part of
it that are prepared) will be translated before the
tribulation, and that there are several stages of the
translation.

The scriptural allusions **to** it are so frequent, that
we scarcely know where to commence our investiga-
tions. In the Psalms, in Isaiah, and the other books
of the Prophets, and in the New Testament, especially the Book of Revelation, we find ample proof.
Though many will fail to perceive it, as the Apostles
failed to understand the Saviour's oft-repeated words,
prior to their reception of the gift of the Holy Spirit.
Yet they were not without fault, or the Saviour would
not have chided them for folly, and slowness of heart,
in failing to perceive all that the prophets had
spoken.

Luke xvii. 34—37 is generally admitted to refer to
the Translation—"I tell you in that night there shall

be two men in one bed; the one shall be taken, and the other left," &c. "And they answered, and said unto him, Where, Lord?" A very natural question for them to ask where they should be taken to. "And He said unto them, wheresover the body is, thither will the eagles be gathered together."

The eagles in this passage are identical with the first translation, and are the same as the flying eagle in Rev. iv. 7. And those that "mount up with wings as eagles," in Isaiah xl. 31.

If we can identify this creature* like a flying eagle in Rev. iv. 7 with Luke xvii. 37 and Isaiah xl. 31, we have a strong argument for the translation before the tribulation.

In Luke it is said, "they shall be taken, and gathered together where the body (Christ) is." In Isaiah, it is said "they that wait† for the Lord, shall mount up *with wings* as eagles." And in Revelation, the creature, like a flying eagle, is *in heaven before the tribulation;* prior to the opening of the Seals, the pouring out of the Last Vials; and all the grand Panorama of the Judgment scenery designated as the Great Tribulation. (Or the tribulation, the great one, as it is in some versions.)

If the eagle translation is in heaven before the commencement of these temporal judgments, it surely does not pass through the tribulation, consequently must have been translated prior to its commencement.

---

* It is translated "beast," in our common version; but in the original it is "being" or "creature."

† It is "them that wait *upon* the Lord," in Isaiah xl. 31. But in the original it is "them that wait *for* the Lord!"

There may be tribulations through which they may pass, but not the great one.

Read the fourth, fifth, and sixth chapters of Revelation consecutively, and you will see that they are in heaven in the fourth and fifth, while the judgments do not commence until the sixth chapter. In the commencement of the fourth, John "beholds a door opened in heaven." He sees the heavenly throne, and Him that sat upon it; and in describing the various parties that he saw, there is a being like a flying eagle among them. This flying eagle is the first translation. Again in that millennial chapter, the 26th of Isaiah, we have in substance the same. It opens with the description of the heavenly city, and the gates are ordered to be opened, (verse 2d,) "that the *righteous nation* may enter." Peter calls the Christian Church a "holy nation," which is the same, of course, as a "righteous nation."

This gives a clue as to who the righteous nation is that is to enter the opened gates into the mansions prepared for them. (John xiv. 2, 3, 28.) And this is prior to the Lord's coming out of *his place*, to punish the inhabitants of the earth for iniquity. (Isaiah xxvi. 1, 21.

They are called into his chambers or mansions for the special purpose of being preserved from "the indignation." "Come thou, my people, into thy chambers for a little while, until the indignation be overpast." (Isaiah xxvi. 20.) Here they are taken away for the express purpose of escaping the indignation which is to be poured out upon the ungodly for their iniquity. Indeed, it would scarcely be mer-

ciful to leave those who had not been partakers of
their sins, to partake of the judgment upon sin.
And why should it be thought a strange thing? We
have seen how Noah's family were removed, and
preserved from the flood, of judgments that came
upon the ungodly at that time; and also how they
were brought back to earth, after it was purified and
cleansed. These things are all types of still greater
events.

It is said, "I have used similitudes by the ministry
of the Prophets." And again, "Whatsoever things
were written aforetime, were written for our learning." (Hosea xii. 10; Rom. xv. 4.)

If corroborative evidence is needed that the righteous nation that enter the open gates, in Isaiah xxvi.
2, is identical with the translation, we have it in the
Judgment scenes that immediately follow, and also
from its connection with the first resurrection. For
immediately after the gates are opened for the
righteous to enter, we have the bringing down of the
high, and the fall of the great cities.

"For He bringeth down them that dwell on high;
the lofty city, he layeth it low; He layeth it low,
even to the ground; He bringeth it even to the dust."
"Yea, in the way of thy judgments we have waited
for thee. . . . . For when thy judgments are in the
earth, the inhabitants of the world will learn righteousness." "For all nations shall come and worship
before thee, when thy judgments are made manifest."
(Isaiah xxvi. 5, 8, 9; Rev. xv. 4.)

This laying of the lofty cities low in Isaiah xxvi. 5,
is identical with the fall of the cities of the nations in

Rev. xvi. 19. This every one admits to be a part of the Tribulation scenes of the last days. We have also an intimation of the removal of the Church, just prior to these events, in the same chapter, Rev. xvi. 15.

These and many other texts fix the date of the entrance of the righteous nation through the open gates at the period of, or just *prior to the tribulation*, or temporal judgments of the last days, when the Gentile kingdoms shall be broken up under the figure of the stone cut out of the mountain, breaking them to pieces together, and the winds carrying them away like chaff on the summer threshing-floor. (Dan. ii. 34, 35.)

Here the Jerusalem type is not only complete in the breaking up of the nations of professing Christendom, as the Jewish Church and State was broken up, (because they sinned against their light,) but the scattering of the chaff to the four winds typifies the scattering of the Gentile nations, as the Jews were scattered into all the world.

As the removal of the Church (as many as are prepared) is the subject of our present remarks, let us recall your attention to the fact, that these lofty cities are laid even with the dust, after the righteous have entered through the open gates, and consequently prior to the Apocalyptic judgments. Let us also again call your attention to the fact, that in the latter part of the same chapter, (26th of Isaiah,) the reason is given why they are called to enter the heavenly mansions at this period. That is, that they may be preserved from the punishment which He "comes out of His place to inflict on the inhabitants of the earth for iniquity." This calling into their chambers for this purpose, is positively identified as the first translation, by its connection with the first resurrection.

Paul says the translated ones shall not go before the first resurrection, but both shall be caught up together. (1 Thess. iv. 16, 17.) Now, if we can establish the fact that there is a resurrection in connection with it, we have positive proof that this translation is to be removed before the indignation, and kept there for a little while, (like Noah's family in the Ark,) until the indignation shall be overpast. In verse 19th we have most unmistakably a resurrection, not of the wicked, for they all sing with joy. "Awake and sing, ye that dwell in dust, ... for the earth shall cast forth her dead." Come, my people, enter thou into thy chambers, and shut thy doors about thee, (as the door of the Ark was shut after Noah entered it,) hide thyself as it were *for a little moment*, until the indignation be overpast. "For behold the Lord cometh out of his place to punish the inhabitants of the earth for iniquity."

There is another event also which identifies this with the first resurrection. It is the punishment of Satan, in the commencement of the 27th chapter of Isaiah, which ought never to have been divided from the 26th chapter.* This is one of the cases where

* It is well known that the Scriptures originally were not divided into chapters and verses. "The dividing of the Old Testament into chapters, as they now stand in our translation, is attributed to Cardinal Hugo, who lived about the middle of the thirteenth century." Robert Stevens, a French printer, had previ-

there is a division of chapters, when there ought scarcely to have been a comma between.

The 26th chapter of Isaiah ends with the announcement that the Lord comes out of his place to punish the inhabitants of the earth for iniquity, and the 27th chapter commences with another judicial punishment at that period, evidently connecting it with the 26th chapter. "In that day the Lord with his sore and great and strong sword, shall punish Leviathan, the piercing serpent, even Leviathan that crooked serpent. And He shall slay the dragon that is in the sea." (Isaiah xxvii. 1.)

Notice the point. "In that day." What day? The day spoken of at the close of the preceding chapter, when he should raise the righteous dead, translate the living, and come out of his place to punish the inhabitants," &c. (Isaiah xxvi. 19, 20, 21.)

ously (1551) divided the New Testament into verses, as they now stand in the various versions.

This division into verses, though very convenient, is not to govern the sense, and there are *several instances in which the sense is injured, if not destroyed, by an improper division.* Very often the chapter breaks off in the midst of a narrative, and if the reader stops because the chapter ends, he loses the connection. (Matt. x. 42; xii. 1. Luke xix. 41–48; xx. 1–8. Acts xxi. 22, 23. Gal. i. 23; ii. 1.) Sometimes the break is altogether in the wrong place, and separates two sentences, which must be taken together to be understood. 1 Cor. xii. 31; xiii. 1. 2 Cor. vi. 18; vii. 1. Ephes. iv. 31, 32; li. 2. Phil. iii. 21; iv. 1.)

☞ Again the verses often divide a sentence into two different paragraphs, when there ought scarcely to be a comma between them. (Luke iii. 21, 22. 2 Cor. vi. 7, &c. 1 Peter i. 3, 4, &c. And sometimes a fragment of a subject is separated from its proper place, and put where it is without any connection." (Coloss. iii. 25; iv. 1.)—" *Sunday School Union Bible Dictionary.*"

Now, compare this punishing of the Serpent, and slaying of the Dragon, in Isaiah xxvii. 1, with the binding of Satan in Rev. xx. 2, and see if it is not identical. Identified by the use of two of the names, "Serpent and Dragon."

Isaiah says that the Lord when he cometh out of his place to punish the inhabitants, shall also punish the Serpent, and slay the Dragon. And John describes the mode of his punishment. "He laid hold on the Dragon, that old Serpent, which is the Devil and Satan, and bound him a thousand years, and cast him into the bottomless pit." (Rev. xx. 2.) The Lord is also mentioned as coming in connection with the binding of Satan, under the figure of an angel coming down from heaven." This angel is undoubtedly the Saviour—identified by the possession of the keys, as we will see by comparing Rev. i. 18 with Rev. xx. 1, 4. And the first resurrection is synchronical. John also shows the manner in which he punishes the inhabitants of the earth for iniquity.

Isaiah announces the fact that he will punish them, but John shows that he really does punish them with "the sore," and great and strong sword, of which Isaiah speaks; and he also shows the result in the complete overthrow and slaughter of Antichrist and his armies in that greatest of battles that ever was, or ever will be fought; where the Beast and the false Prophet are captured, and "cast alive into a lake of fire, burning with brimstone, and the remnant were slain with the sword." (Rev. xix. 20, 21.) There are many passages in the Psalms which are read daily without even an inquiry into their meaning.

Such as the following:—"For in the time of (the) trouble, He shall hide me in His pavilion; in the secret of His tabernacle shall he hide me." "Then shall mine head be lifted up above mine enemies round about me." . . . . . "Thou shalt hide them in the secret of thy presence; . . . . . thou shalt keep them secretly in a pavilion from the strife." . . . . . "For thou art my hiding place; thou shalt preserve me from the trouble." "For this shalt every one that is godly pray in a time when thou mayest be found. Surely in the floods of great waters thou shalt not come nigh me." "They that were ready went into the marriage, and *the door was shut*. Now when the Master is once risen up, and *shut to the door*, ye may stand without, and cry in vain." Psalms xxvii. 5, 6; xxxi. 20; xxxii. 6, 7. Matt. xxv. 10.

By taking Paul's rule, comparing Scripture with Scripture, we may gather some very valuable truths from the above Scriptures. A part of these have been partially and typically fulfilled in God's dealings with his ancient people.

But the principal part of it is yet to be fulfilled. Let us give these texts a more particular examination. What "time of trouble" is this from which He is to "hide them in His pavilion?" Notice, it is in His pavilion. Where is His pavilion but in the heavens? It is said in Isaiah xxvi. 20, " Hide thyself for a little while until the indignation be overpast;" and in these passages from the Psalms, the same hiding is mentioned, and they are hid in the time of the trouble or tribulation. They are not hid in some of the hiding places of the earth; "they are *raised up*," and hid in His pavilion "in the secret of His presence, in His tabernacle" or dwelling.

And this is in the time of the trouble.

There is one point that we particularly wish to notice,—that they are commanded to pray for the translation. "For this shall every one that is godly pray." It is not the ungodly praying for salvation, but the godly praying for translation; as is shown in the next verse, by the mention of the hiding-place, and preservation in the time of trouble, and as we see in the preceding verses of the 31st Psalm, which ought not to have been divided into a separate chapter from the 32d. (Psalm xxxi. 32, xx. 21. Psalm xxxii. 6, 7.) In Psalm xxxii. 21, the strong city is mentioned; (the same as the city in Isaiah xxvi. 1.) This is another point of identity, in evidence that this time of trouble from which he preserves them, by hiding them in his pavilion, is the same as that in Isaiah xxvi. 21,—"Yea in the Shadow of thy wings will I make my refuge, until these calamities be overpast." "For he shall send from heaven and save me." (Psalm v. 7—i. 6.) Here we see that "He sends from Heaven to save them, and provides a refuge in the shadow of his wings until these calamities be overpast." Or, as Isaiah has it, "until the indignation be overpast." And this was in a time, when his soul was among those who were as lions, representing under this figure their fierceness, and destructiveness. He also mentions, that at the time of his deliverance he was among men who were set on fire, (a fit emblem of

Spiritualists, who are possessed with demoniac spirits, by whose agency much of the tribulation of the last days will be brought in.) "Their teeth were as spears, and they had prepared a net for his steps and digged a pit, into which they fell themselves," (as they finally will, at the Battle of Armageddon.)

The net they had prepared, is also mentioned in Psalms xxxi. 4, (the same chapter in which it is said they are preserved in the time of trouble), and in this Psalm he prays to be pulled out of the net, and for speedy deliverance. (Psalm xxxi. 1, 4.)

In Psalm lvii. 1, 8, he speaks of deliverance as a certainty. "He shall send down from heaven, and save them from the reproach (or persecution) of him that would swallow them up."

If there is a refuge provided in which they are preserved until the tribulation calamities are past, they surely do not pass through them, and consequently are translated before the tribulation.

In Psalm lvii. we see that "He sends down from Heaven, and saves them from those that would swallow them up, and preserves them in a place of refuge until these calamities are past." Immediately after, in Psalm lviii. we see his punishment of the wicked. They are mentioned as "melting away as waters, and as cut to pieces, and as being taken away as with a whirlwind." "And this in the time when God judgeth in the earth."

"The righteous are to rejoice when they see this vengeance, and to wash their feet in the blood of the wicked." "So that a man shall say verily there is a reward for the righteous, there is a God that judgeth in the earth." (Psalm lviii. 10, 11.) Now we wish to make a few remarks here, on the seeming spirit of revenge that David expresses in these passages, but which is not David at all, and has no reference to his personal retaliations, but does expressly refer to the judgments of God upon Antichrist and his armies in the last days.

The whole passage ends, with "verily there is a God that judgeth in the earth." The rejoicing of the righteous here, is not because they felt any revengeful feelings towards even these hardened sinners, who were persecuting everything that is good, and destroying all who would not unite in their false worship. It is in the period when Antichrist is in the full tide of his destroying power, and after he has proclaimed that all that would not worship the image of the Beast should be killed, both small and great, rich and poor, free and bond, &c., &c. And at the time when the Saviour comes to destroy him and "them that destroy the earth," and to give reward to His servants. (Rev. xi. 17, 18.) The righteous are represented as rejoicing and giving thanks that he has taken to himself his great power.

And well may they rejoice in the setting up of His peaceable kingdom. "For He shall execute judgment and righteousness in the earth." "Behold a King shall reign in righteousness." "And thine eyes shall see thy King in his beauty." "Then shall the moon be confounded, and the sun shall be ashamed, when the Lord of hosts shall reign in Mount Zion, and in Jerusalem, before His Ancients gloriously." "And the ransomed of the Lord shall return and come unto Zion, with songs and everlasting joy upon their heads; and they shall obtain joy and gladness, and sorrow and sighing shall flee away," "violence shall no more be heard in thy land, nor wasting, nor destruction within thy borders." "I will also make thy officers peace, and thine exactors righteousness." "Thy people shall all be righteous, and they shall inherit the land together." "Thy sun shall no more go down .... for the Lord shall be thine everlasting light, and the days of thy mourning shall be ended." "For behold, I create a new heavens and a new earth." "Be ye glad and rejoice *forever* in that which I create." To this command, to rejoice forever in these new and transcendently beautiful creations, and the prosperous and peaceful Kingdom which His reign will bring in, they respond, "We give thee thanks, O Lord God Almighty, which art, and wast, and art to come, because thou hast taken unto thee thy great power, and reigned." "For the nations are angry, and thy wrath is come, and the time of the dead, that they should be judged, and that thou shouldst give reward to thy servants . . . and shouldst destroy them that destroy the earth." (Rev. xi. 15— 18; Psalms lvii. and lviii; Jer. xxxiii. 15—17; Jer. xxiii. 5—7; Isaiah xxxii. 1; Isaiah xxxiii. 17—22, 24; Isaiah xxxv. 10; Isaiah lxv. 17, 18.)

Who would not rejoice that such a destroyer should be destroyed. Better one than many.

For it will come to this, the destruction of all the righteous, unless their destroyer himself should be destroyed. "For except that day should be short-ened, there should be no flesh saved; but for the elect's sake those days shall be shortened." This prophecy was partially and typically fulfilled at the destruction of Jerusalem; but will have its antitype and more complete fulfilment in the breaking up of Gentile Christendom.

Properly understood then, these passages in the Psalms and the Prophets, that seem to invoke vengeance, have nothing to do with personal passions or resentments, but by studying the context carefully, we will in almost every case find they refer to the Judicial dealings of God with his enemies in the last days.

He is long-suffering, and forbears as long as it is safely possible. Men will become wholly impervious to good in the last days through demoniacal possessions, similar to those in the Saviour's time; who are in fact, destroying demons entering men, changing their natures into instruments of destruction, and divesting them of human sympathies, and affections, so that all appeals for mercy from their helpless victims will be in vain. Their mission is to gather the whole world to battle. (Rev. xvi. 14.) And they will "succeed in seducing many from the faith." 1 Timothy iv. 1—3.

They are now busily at their work, and are far advanced in their demoniacal mission; implanting fierce passions, which may break out in a volcanic irruption of war at any moment, in which the nations and kingdoms may go down in a sea of blood. The slain are mentioned at that day, as "lying from one end of the earth even to the other end of the earth;"

17

"and few men left." It is said to be such a time of trouble as never was, or ever will be again.

And shall it be said that there is anything contrary to Christian spirit or principle, in rejoicing that the destroying power of such a monster has come to an end, and that the kingdom of righteousness and peace is set up in its place.

Let David, then, be vindicated from any such personal feelings,—for he speaks, not the language of personalities, but of Prophecy, in reference to the fate of Antichrist and his destroying armies in the last days.

The passage in Psalm lviii. 10, where the righteous are said to wash their feet in the blood of their enemies, appears very revengeful, until we examine it in connection with corresponding passages. This is at the period of The Great Slaughter, when the towers shall fall, and "blood shall come even unto the horses' bridles for the space of a thousand and six hundred furlongs." Isaiah xxx. 25—33, Rev. xiv. 20.

Viewed in this light, we can see that it will be a natural consequence and necessity that the feet of the righteous should be bathed in the blood of the wicked, if their feet touch earth at all—and not as any act of retaliation on their part. And the same with the wicked, being ashes under the soles of their feet (in Malachi iv. 3,) as some of them surely will be burned in the last days, and therefore will be ashes under the soles of their feet. It is not the wicked people, so much as their wicked acts that David prays may come to an end, as in the following passage. "O *let the wickedness* of the wicked *come to an end.*"

"If he turn not, He will whet his sword, He hath bent his bow and made it ready." (Psalm vii. 9, 12.) The men upon whom David invokes these chastisements were of the most callous character, and totally impervious to any good. "Their poison is like the poison of a serpent. They are like the deaf adder that stoppeth her ear; which will not hearken to the voice of the charmers, charming never so wisely." (Psalm lviii. 4, 5.) Their character, as expressed in this passage, evinces the very extreme of malignant wickedness; and also shows them to be so determinedly hardened, as to be impervious to all godly influences, turning a deaf ear to all who would lead them to reformation or righteousness, "charm they never so wisely."

Think of the character of a serpent; and then see, if a figure of more hardened wickedness, and cunning deception, could have been chosen to represent the brutal and hopeless state into which they had sunk. Who ever knew a serpent to show an emotion of affection, or to make any grateful return for kindness? Who ever knew them to possess one good quality, that any one could respect or admire? Almost all other animals have been tamed, and show something like a grateful appreciation of kindness; and when brought up within the influences of civilization, the most ferocious in their natures have been tamed. The serpent of all other animals, remains hopelessly malignant, and will remain so until the end; and is in this an appropriate type of the malignant character of Satan, who remains unreclaimed and irreclaimable, even after a thousand years punishment and confinement in the bottomless pit, as is shown by the war which he incites, immediately on his release.

The serpent is also an appropriate figure of those who shall be demoniacally possessed at this period, not only in their malignant disposition to injure without a cause, but in the nature of the injuries that they will succeed in inflicting. "Their poison is like the poison of a serpent." (Psalm lviii. 4.) What could be more deadly than the poison of a serpent? We can imagine nothing, humanly speaking, beyond it.

Of such a character will be the men who will compose the army of Antichrist, and be the chief actors in bringing in the great persecution of the last days, in that "time of trouble such as never was, and never will be." No one need expect any mercy from men so callously wicked—whose malignity can only be fitly compared to the poisonous virus of a serpent; and whose imperviousness to all appeals for mercy can only be likened to the deafness of the deaf adder, who stoppeth her ears. The better the people are, the more they will persecute them, for nothing can equal their hatred of goodness. Lactantius says, "this is the period in which righteousness will be cast out, and innocence detested. For Antichrist will persecute the righteous people; and then shall there be pressure and trial, such as never has been from the beginning of the world. They who reject his mark shall either fly to the mountains, or be siezed and put to death with exquisite torments. He shall also roll up righteous men in the Books of the Prophets, and so burn them."

"And it shall be given him to desolate the world for forty and two months," (three and a half years.)

Cyril, Bishop of Jerusalem, says, "Satan will use this person (Antichrist) as an instrument, personally acting in him. *At first he will assume the appearance of Philanthropy*, but afterwards will show himself full of stern severity, especially towards the people of God." Gregory Nazianzen says, "Antichrist shall come for the desolation of the world." Irenæus says, "Antichrist shall lay waste all things in this world." It was a common tradition among the fathers, that Antichrist should first come, and desolate the whole world, and then Christ should come and restore all things. He is called "the Desolator." I regret that we have not space to add numerous other testimonies from the ancient fathers, equally valuable, nor to comment upon the myriads of other evils and sufferings of that fearful time.

From all these the first translation will be preserved, by being removed to the Pavilion Ark before their commencement. From which, those Christians who will be left behind might also be preserved, but for neglect of duty. "For that servant that knew his Lord's will, and did it not, neither prepared himself, shall be beaten with many stripes." And if saved at all—"Saved so as by fire." Luke xii. 40, 47; 1 Cor. iii. 15.

The sufferings to be endured during these fiery trials may well be compared to fire. Prophetic expositors say that the reign of terror in Paris was only a miniature type of what it will be all over the world, in the Great Tribulation, from which there will be "no way of escape, and no place to flee." For the same perils will be everywhere; and those who attempt to escape will only flee from danger to danger. As in the French Reign of Terror, of which, as an able expositor remarks, "the people slaughtered one another in feuds, insurrections, and civil wars, and exterminated with the dagger, the bayonet, and the guillotine, all the influential ranks.

It might be fitly called a national tragedy, and its antitype, which is now approaching, may be called the world's tragedy, in which each nation will be a stage, and every man a tragedian; for the slain of the Lord shall be at that day, from one end of the earth even to the other end of the earth. (Jer. xxv. 33; Isaiah lxvi. 16.) In the city of Paris alone twenty thousand persons perished from starvation, in their hiding places, for fear of assassination if they went out to seek food.

Think of the nearness of a similar reign of terror, intensified a hundred-fold by untold evils, in which all nations will be in this fearful condition.

Will nothing cause the unreflecting multitude to pause and ponder, ere they rush unconsciously into this mad vortex of crime and ruin. Crimes so excessive, and a ruin so fearful, that we can find no parallel only in the faintly shadowed types of the past of crime, whose lessons and warnings seem powerless to stay the rapidly approaching crisis. But it is still more astonishing that Christians, who read and believe that these terrific scenes are right at hand, are so little affected by it, and still conform in part to the world; and while thus conforming to the world, are under the delusion that they will escape the world's chastisement. They acknowledge it to be a duty to circulate the knowledge of these things as much as possible; yet they do not deny themselves to be enabled to do so. They still think they must have the latest style of bonnet, and change of dress fabrics, and in other things must look like other people.

All this has no scriptural warrant. We must be a peculiar people, and not conformed to the world. We must deny ourselves, and take up a daily cross. And if we are not doing this, and not working for this cause, we are not in a state of preparation; and must share the chastisement of that servant that prepared not himself.

For to know and believe that Christ is coming, and yet live as though we did not, is to believe in vain, and will only subject us to many stripes, while that servant that knew not his Lord's will, and yet did commit things worthy of stripes, shall be beaten with few stripes.

We have not touched upon a large portion of the evidence that we find in the Scriptures in reference to the removal of the Church before the Apocalyptic judgments, for want of space, nor can we give the proofs of the several translations. We must defer that until we can write the second part, in which we will endeavor to do justice to the subject. We have scarcely touched upon the proofs given by others, and consequently have left out some of the strongest arguments. For which we refer you to Dr. Seiss's chapter on "*The Two Stages of the Translation,*" in his "*Last Times,*" page 349. And also to Dr. Reinke's able articles in "*The Prophetic Times,*" "*The Eagles,*" and other pieces, which you will find under the signature of "E. E. R."; and Mr. Baxter's two works, "*Napoleon and Armageddon,*" and "*The Coming Battle.*"

Lightning Source UK Ltd.
Milton Keynes UK
UKHW010758011218
333025UK00005B/301/P